Delhi
3 Orangzeb Road

MANSIONS AT DUSK
The Havelis of Old Delhi

MANSIONS AT DUSK
The Havelis of Old Delhi

Text
PAVAN K. VARMA
Photographs
SONDEEP SHANKAR

SPANTECH PUBLISHERS PVT LTD

First published 1992
Published in India by
Spantech Publishers Pvt Ltd
35/33 West Patel Nagar
New Delhi 110008

Published in England by
Spantech Publishers
Spantech House, Lagham Road
South Godstone, Surrey RH9 8HB

ISBN 81-85215-14-6

Typeset in Palatino by
Spantech Publishers Pvt Ltd, New Delhi
and printed at Thomson Press (I) Ltd

To
SATISH JACOB
and
AMRITA KUMAR

Contents

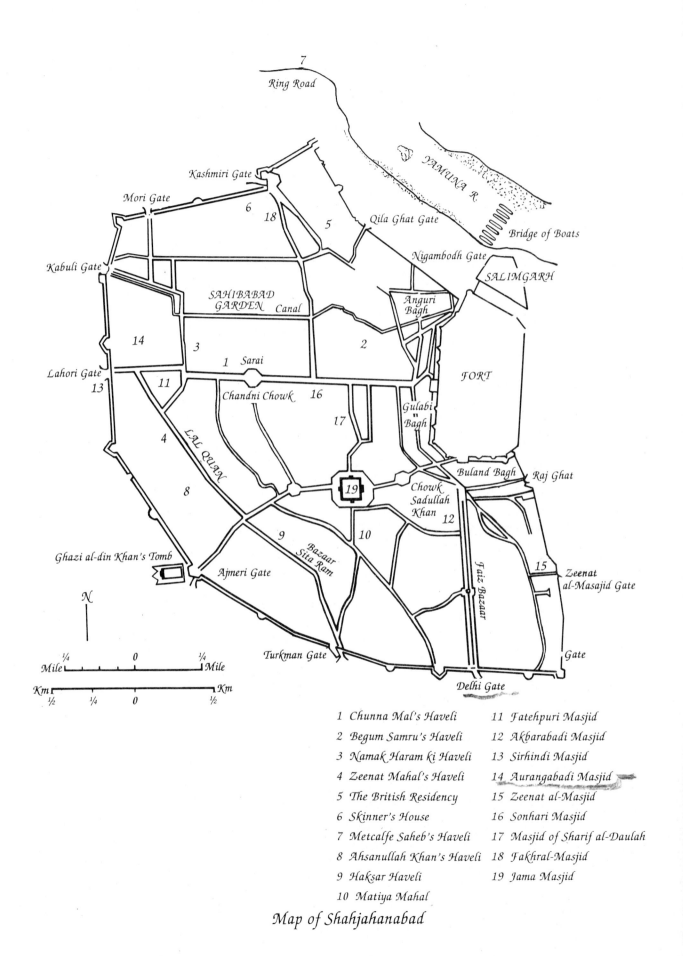

Map of Shahjahanabad

1 Chunna Mal's Haveli
2 Begum Samru's Haveli
3 Namak Haram ki Haveli
4 Zeenat Mahal's Haveli
5 The British Residency
6 Skinner's House
7 Metcalfe Saheb's Haveli
8 Ahsanullah Khan's Haveli
9 Haksar Haveli
10 Matiya Mahal

11 Fatehpuri Masjid
12 Akbarabadi Masjid
13 Sirhindi Masjid
14 Aurangabadi Masjid
15 Zeenat al-Masjid
16 Sonhari Masjid
17 Masjid of Sharif al-Daulah
18 Fakhral-Masjid
19 Jama Masjid

Preface

There is something hauntingly sad in a once beautiful city crumbling away. Shahjahanabad is such a city and it is being destroyed at a relentless pace. Handsome buildings of considerable historicity are demolished routinely. Carved ceilings in wood are ripped off for firewood. Marble stepped-wells are cemented to build godowns. Intricately worked stone pillars are junked to create space for lathes. Gateways and arches, *baolis* and *jaffries*, pillars and panels, seen today, are gone the next.

Indeed, the metamorphosis is so rapid and final that this book could be one of the last attempts to chronicle what once was *through* what remains today. It is a truism to say that Indians have no sense of history. Their vision of the past usually begins with the golden age of the Guptas and ends with the great Mughals. History at his doorstep means very little to the average person overwhelmed by the basic concerns of housing, employment, food and water. Government agencies, enjoined upon to protect historical monuments, are constrained by weak and inadequate laws, and a paucity of funds and trained personnel. There is also the apathy not uncommon to developing societies, in transition, grappling with more immediate priorities. The pity is that once a building is demolished or mutated, the past disappears without a trace. History may repeat itself, historical buildings do not. Under the crush of municipal preoccupations, memories are inevitably short. The new buildings that come upon the debris of the old do not wish to remember the past.

The need to take action to preserve what remains has an emphatic urgency to it. The historic Kotwali of Chandni Chowk was pulled down only a few months ago. Lala Chunna Mal's haveli could soon become a commercial complex. Bhagirath Place, once the palace of Begum Samru, may well undergo a similar fate. Nawab Ali Jaan's haveli, thought to be one of the better preserved homes in the old city, was to have a mutilating partition wall built right through its centre, a week after we visited it: the examples go on and on.

And yet, not all the neglect and spoilage have obliterated the charms of Shahjahanabad. For here, the past still lives with the present in the most enticing ways, which is what made the researching and writing of this book its own reward. The idea first came to my mind when I used to frequent Shahjahanabad for my first book on Ghalib and his times. When I mooted the project to Sondeep Shankar, I found in him an enthusiastic supporter. Then every weekend, for a year, he and I would be in the *galis* of Shahjahanabad, recoiling against the desecration all around, but discovering also the beauty and architectural elegance amidst the over-burgeoning squalor.

Sondeep and I have been 'arrested' by occupants of havelis who suspected us to be 'agents' of rival claimants to the property. Access to the havelis was not always easy. Days of careful spadework would precede the attempt to take pictures. Sometimes, access would be suddenly denied. When we began, we had no idea the adventure this book would prove to be. But such obstacles notwithstanding, there were always compensations which only Shahjahanabad can offer. The warmth and hospitality of the people who readily offered us assistance, the pace and rhythm which only a historical city can have, the lunches at Parathewali Gali or at Karim's—all of these would allow us only reluctantly to return to our synthetic existence in New Delhi.

This book also seeks to resurrect the flavour of an era gone by. It seeks to profile a time when Shahjahanabad, although in decay, was still pre-eminently a residential city, with gardens and canals and pavilions, a manageable population, and a *tehzib* and culture distinctly its own. Our focus has been on havelis of the last century, since almost nothing remains of mansions of greater antiquity. During this period the city may not have had the resplendence of the days of Shah Jahan but an ambience of grace and refinement still persisted in its alleys and streets, its *katras*, *kuchas* and *mohallas*, and above all in the citadels of its feudal elite—the havelis.

Our very special thanks go to Satish Jacob, the integral Delhiwallah, who helped us to identify the havelis, and more important, helped us gain access to them. Although Satish was always hard-pressed for time, we had a strong suspicion that he was enjoying the entire proceedings more than us, and was grateful to us for having kept him from his work. Among the many gracious people in Shahjahanabad who helped make this book possible, we are particularly indebted to Naseem Khan and his family and to Saeed Khan. We are also grateful to Anand Prasad, a descendant of Lala Chunna Mal, for access to his ancestral haveli, and to Dr Raja Ramanna for arranging for us to photograph Metcalfe House. A very warm word of gratitude is due to Amrita Kumar who helped nurture and mould the book in the all-important early stages. To V. Narayanan, my most efficient Secretary, who typed the manuscript in his spare time, what can I say, except as always: 'Thank you, Narayanan'.

This book would have served its purpose if it can jolt the conscience of even a handful of people on the need to preserve and protect the heritage of Shahjahanabad. Some work, notably by the Conservation Society, is being done, but much more needs to be done. I have seen residents in the older quarters of Rome repair the walls of their house in such a manner that a part of the original brick-work, which establishes the antiquity of the house, continues to show. Unless such a pride also infuses the citizens of Delhi, Shahjahanabad will one day simply cease to exist. In its place would be a vast and nondescript commercial slum, and the soul of the city would say with Ghalib:

> If Ghalib continues to weep this way,
> then 'O' people of this world,
> Watch these settlements,
> they will be barren one day.

August 1991
New Delhi

Pavan K. Varma

Introduction

لگتا نہیں ہے جی مرا اُجڑے دیار میں

کس کی بنی ہے عالم ناپائیدار میں

My heart no longer finds solace
Amidst these ruins crumbling;
Whose will has been able to prevail
In this world so fleeting.

Bahadur Shah Zafar

Shah Jahan (1592–1666), the founder of Shahjahanabad.

IT IS NOT entirely clear why Shah Jahan, the great Mughal Emperor, left Agra, the city chosen by his imperial forbears to be the capital of the Mughal empire. More than one reason has been ascribed. One contemporary traveller has argued that 'the excessive heat to which that city (Agra) is exposed during the summer rendered it unfit for the residence of a monarch'.[1] But Delhi in summer could not have been much cooler than Agra. Another historian has opined that the climate of Delhi in general was more healthy. The shortage of space in the Agra Fort, the narrowness of the streets in the city, and the inconvenience caused to the inhabitants by the troops, elephants and the retinues of the emperor and his *umaras*, are some of the other reasons offered to explain the move. The truth appears to be that Shah Jahan left the city where he had reigned for eleven years and where his beloved wife Mumtaz Mahal was buried, because he could not restrain the urge to build a new capital to which he could give his own name. And only Delhi, the mistress of centuries of imperial endeavour, could provide a truly legitimate setting to this aspiration.

The site for the new city, and the red sandstone palace that would dominate it, was chosen with care, with the river Jamuna

12

binding it on the east and the ridge defining it on the west. Astrologers were consulted on the most auspicious day for the inauguration. In conformity with a bizarre but long standing practice, the decapitated bodies of several criminals were interred in the foundation as a sacrifice. Construction began on 12 May 1639. A little over nine years later, Shah Jahan arrived at the head of a magnificent retinue, with his favourite son Prince Dara Shikoh, showering gold and silver along the way, to hold his first court at the Diwan-i-Aam.

The emperor's first concern was to give the fledgling city security. A wall enclosing the city was built—a shoddy job, executed much too quickly—in four months. Made of mud, it did not withstand the onslaught of the monsoon the very next year. A new wall was commissioned and this one took seven years to build, costing a princely sum of four lakh rupees. It was 6664 yards in circumference, with 27 bastions and 14 gates.

A second prerequisite was an assured supply of water. Soon after construction began on the Red Fort, Shah Jahan ordered his engineers to renovate a disused canal built in the fourteenth century by Firuz Shah Tughlaq, which tapped the waters of the river Jamuna. In Akbar's reign the canal had been brought up to Hansi near Hissar. Ali Mardan Khan, Shah Jahan's Persian 'comptroller of works', extended it to Delhi. One branch flowed down Chandni Chowk and thence to Faiz Bazaar. Smaller channels took the water to other important arteries of the city. A second branch, after flowing through several gardens, reached the Red Fort at its north-eastern corner, and its waters were raised to the level of the fort through an in-

A bird's-eye view of Shahjahanabad, showing the bridge of boats across the river Jamuna.

OVERLEAF:
The Jama Masjid.

13

The Chandni Chowk as it was. The Nahar-i-Bihisht can also be seen.

genious mechanism called *shutrgulu* (camel's neck). For the citizens of Delhi, the canal lived up to its name—Nahar-i-Bihisht (Stream of Paradise). Quite apart from the utilitarian aspect of providing a perennial source of sweet water, it gave to Shahjahanabad a coolness and a greenery that made it unique among the cities of India.

Having made provisions for security and water, Shah Jahan encouraged members of his nobility to build their own mansions or havelis. Land had been allotted to the leading *amirs* when the foundations of the palace were laid. Their havelis came up in the crevices and spaces between the principal fixed features of the city. Shah Jahan had a genuine fondness for buildings. Often during his daily darbar, the subject of discussion used to be the mansions being constructed in the city by members of his court. On occasion he would even visit the sites himself. With this degree of royal interest, there was, in the nobility, a desire to outdo each other in architectural novelty and splendour in order to catch the emperor's eye.

However, Shahjahanabad had not been conceived of as a 'residential' city. It was primarily a statement of imperial intention in stone, brick and mortar. Its configuration was assertively 'monumental', with the palace fortress disproportionately dominating the cityscape. A deep moat, stocked with fish, surrounded the ramparts of the Red Fort on the city side. Beyond the moat was a large garden, 'filled at all times with flowers and green shrubs, which, contrasted with the stupendous red walls, produce a beautiful effect'.[2] Next to the garden was a great square where met the most celebrated streets of the city—Chandni Chowk and Faiz Bazaar.

Chandni Chowk stretched from the Lahori Gate of the Red Fort

to the Fatehpuri Mosque. The lovely Nahar-i-Bihisht flowed through the centre of this street-lined avenue. The name Chandni Chowk (Silver or Moonlight Square) came perhaps from the silvery reflection of the moon in a pool built by Shah Jahan's sister, Jahanara, about half way down the street. Adjoining the pool was a beautiful *sarai* (inn) also built by Jahanara. Originally, however, what is now known as Chandni Chowk had several distinct segments. The section from the Lahori Gate of the fort to the Dariba was known as Urdu Bazaar. This colourful bazaar, meaning 'camp market' (referred to in some early accounts as Lahori Bazaar), catered to the needs of the imperial retinue—soldiers, clerks and artisans—residing within the fort. The section west of Dariba, to the Kotwali (City Magistrate's Office), was called Phul ki Mandi or Flower Sellers' Market. The area from here up to Jahanara's Chowk was called Ashrafi Bazaar or Jauhari Bazaar (Jewellers' Market). The last section from Jahanara's Chowk to the Fatehpuri Mosque was called Fatehpuri Bazaar. Chandni Chowk was both a social pivot and a commercial centre. People gathered under the shade of its trees, or along the waters of the canal, or lingered in its many coffee houses, as a matter of daily routine. But above the social chatter and bonhomie, business went on uninterrupted. Contrary to popular belief Chandni Chowk was never a prestigious residential area. Shops were located in the brick arcade that ran down a considerable segment of the street. Behind them were the merchant's warehouses:

The houses of the merchants are built over these warehouses, at the back of the arcades: they look handsome enough from the street, and appear

17

tolerably commodious within; they are airy, at a distance from the dust, and communicate with the terrace-roofs over the shops, on which the inhabitants sleep at night; the rich merchants have their dwellings elsewhere, to which they retire after the hours of business.[3]

Two other important, if less prestigious bazaars which were planned into the city, were Faiz Bazaar and Khas Bazaar. The first ran at right angles to Chandni Chowk, from the Akbarabadi Gate of the city to the fort. The Nahar-i-Bihisht flowed through this bazaar as well. Khas Bazaar connected the Delhi Gate of the fort to the Jama Masjid. At its centre was the famous Sadullah Chowk, which competed with Chandni Chowk in commercial prestige. The colour and spectacle of these bazaars was fabled. Merchants, astrologers, quacks specializing in problems relating to virility, *dastangos* (story-tellers), courtesans and kababwallahs, jostled with each other in a seemingly never ending buzz of activity.

By the middle of the eighteenth century, Delhi boasted of as many as forty-six commercial bazaars. But this did not make it into a kind of extended commercial mart. Shahjahanabad had gardens, lovingly laid out by members of the royal family or by leading members of the nobility. The Mughals brought their weakness for the royal pleasure garden from the heights of Samarqand, and sought to recreate such a retreat in the heat and dust of the plains of northern India. It has been argued that the basic inspiration for these elaborate gardens was Koranic:

The Quran promised each Muslim, as a reward for faithful and steadfast worship of Allah, a place in the heavenly paradise. And paradise, in the

ABOVE:

The walls of Shahjahanabad.

BELOW:

Jahanara's serai in Chandni Chowk. The pool built by her, and from which the main street perhaps derived its name, is also visible.

18

ABOVE:

The Qudsia Bagh.

OVERLEAF:

The steps leading up to the Jama Masjid.

Quran and Islamic tradition, was conceived of as a garden. Thus, for the pious Muslim the earthly garden served as a reminder of his eventual destination, and no matter how large, lush, or richly appointed it might be, it paled beside his own vision of the heavenly garden-paradise he was to inhabit after death.[4]

This being as it may, the fact is that Jahanara took away 50 acres of the walled city to lay her paradise garden—Sahibabad. This garden, just north of Chandni Chowk, was nurtured by the waters of the Nahar-i-Bihisht. There were fountains, waterfalls, pools and a *baradari* (garden pavilion) where, cooled by the surrounding spray of water and sheltered in the deep shadows of luscious trees, she found, in complete privacy, a respite from the travails of summer. Other important gardens were laid just outside the city walls. The Tis Hazari Bagh, full of neem trees, was laid by Shah Jahan outside the Kabuli Gate. Roshanara Begum, daughter of Shah Jahan, built a large garden outside the Lahori Gate, in the area now called Subzi Mandi. Shalimar Bagh, some 6 miles to the north of the city, was constructed by Bibi Akbarabadi, one of the wives of Shah Jahan. Aurangzeb crowned himself emperor in this garden, and much later it was the pleasure retreat of more than one British resident. A particularly well known garden of the eighteenth century was the handiwork of Qudsia Begum, wife of Emperor Mohammad Shah. Known as Qudsia Bagh, it was laid out just outside the Kashmiri Gate. The last Mughal King, Bahadur Shah Zafar, inspite of his penury, continued the tradition and laid out a garden outside the Red Fort and another near Shahdara.

It is not coincidental that so many of these gardens, both known and less known, were in the suburbs. For one, the growing congestion inside the walled city made endeavours like Sahibabad increasingly difficult. For another, a great many havelis were initially located outside the walled city, along the river front, both to the north and south of the palace fortress. Thus, the many gardens and fruit orchards merged and complimented the lush garden estates surrounding the havelis, so that there was a wide swath of cultivated green surrounding the city walls, specially on its northern side, and to the west, up to the shrub and jungles that comprised the rocky incline of the Ridge.

Sarai's were another integral part of the city. The motivation for their construction too was part pragmatic and part spiritual. A place where visitors could find lodging and rest was a genuine need, especially as Delhi attracted a great many merchants and scholars, some from very far off places. Sarais were constructed to earn the *duaen* or recurrent blessings of one's fellow beings. The most magnificent sarai in the city was again the work of the redoubtable Jahanara. Located off Chandni Chowk and adjacent to Sahibabad, her sarai was a magnificent two-storey structure containing ninety rooms. The building was imposing enough for Bernier to list it, alongwith the Jama Masjid, as one of the two most striking structures in the city. A second sarai was built by Nawab Fatehpuri Begum, one of the wives of Shah Jahan. It was located at the end of Chandni Chowk, near the Fatehpuri Mosque also constructed by her.

Among mosques, of which there were many in the city, the Jama Masjid stood unquestioned in its primacy. Shah Jahan began its construction in 1650, very soon after he had taken up residence in the city. With 5000 masons, labourers and stone-cutters working daily, construction took six years and cost ten lakh rupees. When completed, the red standstone soaring minarets and spatial grandeur of the mosque faced with equanimity the imperial might of the Red Fort to the east. The Jama Masjid became the hub of Shahjahanabad. Every afternoon, on the steps leading down from its southern gateway, towards Chitli Qabar, an impromptu bazaar came up, in which the sale of birds was a special attraction. Jugglers and story-tellers assembled on the steps of its northern gateway. For the dastangos, the most popular narratives were the Persian classics: *Dastan-e-Amir Hamza*, *Qissa-i-Hatim Tai* and *Dastan-e-Bostan-e-Khayal*. A massive Gudri Bazaar (flea market) was held in front of the central gateway facing the fort. 'A Gudri-Bazaar is held here every day and a thousand varieties of clothes are displayed. Besides, beautiful birds and other curiosities are exhibited. Horses as well as pigeons are sold in this market.'[5]

It is estimated that over a hundred mosques were constructed in the first hundred years of the life of the city. By 1857 there were two hundred. The better known of these were, on a similar but smaller scale, focal points of the city in their own right, for instance the Fatehpuri, Akbarabadi, Sirhindi and Sonari masjids. *Musafir khanas*, *madrasas* and hospitals tended to come up around the more prominent mosques, reinforcing their crucial role in the city profile. There were temples too; the most well known was the Jain temple in Mohalla Dharampura which was built over eight years (1800–8) at a cost of five lakh rupees.

Within this scheme, the havelis of the great and rich played a subsidiary role. It was only later that they became foci of self-sustaining importance. A much more distinctive aspect of the city

RIGHT:

Nau Ghara, or the street with nine houses, is a typical kucha off Chandni Chowk.

OVERLEAF:

An intricately carved arched gateway announcing a haveli.

'Lahori' bricks, commonly used in the old city, criss-crossed in the making of an arch.

was the development of vocational quarters such as Nil Katra, Kucha Chini Wala, or Chamar ka Hata (the areas of wax workers, sugar traders and leather workers). There was no fixed residential area for the mansions of the rich; they were scattered in the many *kuchas*, *katras*, *mohallas* and *galis*, that came up as the city grew and evolved, coexisting with equanimity with both the architecturally grandiose and the penuriously unpretentious. Perhaps for the fastidious, this coexistence of havelis with the mud and thatch houses of the poorer sections, disturbed the city profile. But apparently the Delhiwallah, be it the nawab or his retainer, did not mind. The havelis were absorbed effortlessly in the overall architectural ambience of the city, subsumed under a cultural homogeneity that integrated its various elements into one composite whole. Although scattered locationally, each haveli tended to create around itself a small township with its own sphere of influence, consisting of the houses and establishments of the members of the nobleman's retinue, a small bazaar catering to the needs of the nawab's household, and an elaborate host of service groups, taking care of the amir's stable, garden, carriages and such like.

It is significant that Hindu and Muslim mansions had little to differentiate them. Havelis, irrespective of the religious persuasion of their patriarch, followed the same essential features, with this difference that sometimes a Hindu *rais* would have a temple near his house, while a Muslim amir, a mosque. Apart from this understandable divergence, havelis at best reflected variations of their owners' personality, not of basic format. There is no account of a foreign observer categorizing the residential mansions of Delhi on a religious basis. The *Gazetteer of Delhi District* (1883–4) noted: 'There is no great difference in the style of houses of Hindus and Muhammadans. The main thing that causes variations is the pecuniary conditions of the house-holders.'[6]

Seen in the context of its own milieu, the haveli was not only the culmination of an aesthetic ideal, but a vigorously functional adaptation of such an aesthetic. Its inspiration was indigenous, giving the impression to an observer that it was not merely located at a certain place, but had evolved from it. The famous French traveller and physician, Bernier, who visited Shahjahanabad in 1663, was struck by precisely this aspect of its buildings, and strongly berated

A scene outside a haveli gateway.

the view point of those who judged architectural elegance, without contextual knowledge:

In treating of the beauty of these towns, I must emphasize that I have sometimes been astonished to hear the contemptuous manner in which Europeans in the Indies speak of these and other places. They complain that the buildings are inferior in beauty to those of the Western world, forgetting that different climates require different styles of architecture; that what is useful and proper at Paris, London or Amsterdam, would be entirely out of place at Delhi; in so much that if it were possible for any one of those great capitals to change place with the metropolis of the Indies, it would become necessary to throw down the greater part of the city, and to rebuild it on a totally different plan. Without doubt, the cities of Europe may boast great beauties; these, however, are of an appropriate character, suited to a cold climate. Thus, Delhi also may possess beauties adapted to a warm climate.[7]

The basic inspiration for all mansions in the city was the Qilla-i-Mualla, the 'Fort of Exalted Dignity'. Of course it was not a model capable of literal emulation; however, the havelis sought to incorporate in themselves its essential elements, because, in a very basic sense, the fort itself was a fort-haveli or a haveli-fort. It had like the havelis, a blank, walled facade. Indeed, for the common man a haveli, in terms of its privacy, was as forbidding as a fortress. It was commonly said that inside a haveli, *parinda bhi par nahin maar sakta hai* (even a bird cannot have access to the inside of the haveli). Similarly, the fort had a 'public' area, gradually withdrawing into a protected private area of family apartments and the *mahalsara* or *zenana* (ladies' apartments); it had within the inner secluded area, gardens and fountains, and carefully nurtured pleasure retreats; it had intricately constructed *hammams* (baths) and even more beautiful *tehkhanas* (basements). The source of water for both the fort and the havelis was the same—the Nahar-i-Bihisht.

If the palace fortress dominated the urban area as a whole, the havelis dominated the areas immediately in their vicinity. These comparisons are not so difficult to understand, once, overcoming the extroverted grandeur of the fort, we appreciate that both the Shahanshah and his prominent citizens were guided by the same

27

The aangan or enclosed
courtyard inside a haveli.

functional imperatives; the scale of construction was vastly different, but the conditioning impulse was similar. Moreover, many of
the royal princes lived outside the fort and naturally sought to
duplicate—albeit on a reduced scale—some of the features of the
fort in their city mansions.

An arched gateway, often richly decorated, was usually the procla-
mation of the existence of a haveli. The ingenious mechanism by
which a perfect arch was constructed merits mention as there were
no concrete load-bearing bricks in those days. 'Lahori' bricks (so
named because they were brought from Lahore) still evident in the
walled city, were criss-crossed so precisely, that the entire balance of
the arch hinged on the accurate placement of a single brick. From
the gateway, leading inwards, was an extended vestibule, or long
passageway. Sometimes this was covered by a low roofway, a *chhatta*,
where the common visitors and retainers would spend a considerable part of their day. A man of substance would have scores of
such hangers on. The greater the hustle and bustle, the greater the
standing of the nawab sahib. At the end of the vestibule, or to one
side of it, there opened another door leading into the haveli proper.
This door usually opened onto a blank wall—the *purdah diwar*. It
prevented visitors from looking right in and reinforced the privacy
of the havelis.

In more imperial constructions, the arched gateway on the outside
led to another gateway inside—the Naqqar Khana or literally the
'House of the Drums', from whose vantage point the drummers,
musicians and trumpeters of the nobleman's household, would
proclaim the four watches of the day, or announce important visitors.

In the Red Fort, the Naqqar Khana was the point at which all visitors, even the British until 1857, would dismount from their horses and proceed on foot. It opened onto a large forecourt (*jilau khana*) with rooms along its sides. These housed the servants and soldiers attached to the mansions. The forecourt was also the area where the palanquin and carriages of visitors or their horses and elephants would await in readiness.

In basic format, havelis had two divisions: an outer area where the amir conducted his official business, entertained visitors and interacted with his staff, and an inner area which constituted the personal living area, the *mahalsarai* and zenana. The *diwan khana* was the most prestigious centre-piece of the public area. In effect it corresponded to the modern drawing-room, but because the amir also held court there, it had an orientation of greater formality. An office and a library were the other important rooms in this segment.

Havelis have been called 'introverted gardens'. The applicability of this expression becomes evident when we look at the planning of the inner-most spaces, the sanctum sanctorum of the secluded mahalsarai. Here, privacy was embellished by apartments and pavilions that nestled amidst exquisitely laid out gardens and pools, fountains and fruit trees. An observer standing outside a haveli would scarcely have reason to believe that behind the forbidding, blank wall, were lovingly indulged areas of light and openness. Even where elaborate formal gardens were not laid, the basic pattern of construction was to have verandahs and rooms around a private open space—the *aangan* (courtyard), *chowk* or *sehan*. It was not unusual to find a huge tree growing even in a small aangan.

ABOVE:
The two-tiered verandah, daalan, dar daalan, opening onto an aangan.

OVERLEAF LEFT:
The purdah diwar, opposite the entrance to a haveli. The diwar provides privacy to the inner quarters of a haveli.

OVERLEAF RIGHT:
Another entrance to a haveli.

29

Care was also taken to ensure that the aangan received a great deal of sunlight. The verandahs surrounding the open chowk were mostly two tiered: the outer verandah (*daalan*), more overtly an accessory to the courtyard, giving way to an inner verandah (*dar. daalan*), less open and more private. This system of daalan and dar daalan allowed the inner daalan to open out into the courtyard through an intermediate space. Abutting the daalan on both sides was often a mezzanine space, the *du chhatthi* or *do hashmi* or *janashin*, from whose vantage point, unseen behind intricately worked *jaafries* or screens, the ladies of the house could witness 'private–public' functions such as a mujra or a music performance.

The haveli made an attempt, at least partially, to accommodate individual privacies within the larger extended family. This was done by adopting the cellular form of construction: one courtyard, with its own rooms and verandah, leading to another courtyard, both linked to each other, yet both enclosing a semi-detached space subsisting on its own. Havelis often extended themselves in an ad hoc manner along this cellular pattern, responding to additions in the family or the need for more space.

Within the mahalsarai, an essential feature was the tehkhana or underground chamber. This was not merely a basement: it was an integral part of the residential quarters, where the entire family would retreat during the long days of summer. Considerable planning, therefore, went into its construction. Firstly, it had to be fairly deep underground in order to remain cool during summer. Secondly, it had to be large enough to accommodate the entire extended family. Thirdly, while obviating direct sunlight, it had to allow some light and air to enter through overhead *roshandans*. Some havelis had more than one tehkhana. The one used by the amir was however the most elaborately and ornately decorated. Safdarjung's tehkhana had marble pillars and fountains, and was 78 ft long and 27 ft wide. A British army officer living in Shahjahanabad in the 1830s in a haveli which he felt 'doubtless belonged at some time, to a man of great wealth' has this description of his tehkhana:

The descent to the apartment was 30 ft, and the surprise and pleasure were equal, to find such beautiful rooms and so elegantly arranged and furnished . . . long corridors lead to different apartments embellished with coloured walls, and other decorations . . . and many exquisite drawings of places of celebrity in Delhi and its neighbourhood, add to the appearance of this truly fairy palace; light is admitted from above and by windows in the eastern face. A retreat of this kind in the hot months of April, May and June is a luxury scarcely to be described. . . .[8]

It was in these tehkhanas that the members of the nobility took shelter from the plunder and massacre unleashed by the British after they recaptured the city in 1857. And it was from these tehkhanas that the British recovered the greatest part of their loot of gold and silver and precious gems.

The tehkhana was not the only refuge against the Indian summer. High ceilings and thick walls served this purpose as well. Bernier paid tribute to this functional sensitivity, when he wrote:

In these hot countries a house is considered beautiful if it be capacious, and if the situation be airy and exposed on all sides to the wind, especially to the northern breezes. A good house has its courtyards, gardens, trees, basins of water, small jets d'eau in the hall or at the entrance, and hand-

some subterraneous apartments which are furnished with large fans and on account of their coolness, are fit places for repose from noon until four or five o'clock, when the air becomes suffocatingly warm.[9]

Terraces were also cleverly planned: they were bereft of awkward architectural appurtenances that would block the much loved *purvaiya*, the wind from the east, that blew crisp and cool in the pre-dawn darkness, or at night, when one lay back on cool, white bed sheets and gazed at the stars above. At the same time, each terrace had to have a privacy of its own, since more than one couple would be sharing the total terrace area. This was done by building the terraces at different levels and on different areas of the roof space. Terraces were particularly popular during the monsoons, when, after the still, unbearable heat of summer, the air would suddenly turn cool, carrying with it the promise of rain. Adjoining the terrace would be a large room, into which the beds could be moved quickly in case of a downpour, or when a dust storm struck unexpectedly, or even if the morning air became unseasonably nippy.

Khus (aromatic fiberous root of Indian grass) screens, kept constantly wet, were used extensively in summer. The ubiquitous *jalis* or stone screens, beautifully worked in geometric patterns, also had a functional role. Through them, air at a micro level could travel from 'cool to hot, establishing currents to induce ventilation in the building, control the harsh light and yet maintain indoor privacy . . . '.[10] Another truly unique innovation was the 'wind catching' shafts that would literally catch currents of air from above and funnel them into the interior of the haveli. These shafts were made by building double walls enclosing a very narrow space. Jutting out above roof level, towards the direction of the breeze, they sucked the air in.

The ultimate structure to dilute the travails of summer was the baradari or garden pavilion. Built on a raised platform in the midst of a garden, it was open to the breeze from all directions and was surrounded by pools of water and fountains. It was the nawab sahib's pride, as it was indeed that of his emperor within the qila. It is difficult to find extant examples of these delicate constructions, but we can get a fairly good idea of their features from a description of their role models, the Sawan and Bhadon pavilions, built in the Red Fort, within the beautiful Hayat Baksh garden:

This Iram-like Hayat Bakhsh garden, which, by the display of its beautiful flower-beds, of the various green plants, and blessed flowers, and by the running water channels facing the garden, in the name of Holy God, *is a garden*. The wave of its fresh grass has surpassed the roses, and the fruitful trees of diverse kinds are interlaced with each other in such a way that the sky is not anywhere visible beneath them. Especially does the tank in its centre, which is 60 gaz by 60 gaz, shine as a sun-like mirror with its waving light, and it is decorated with 49 silver jets, besides 112 more jets which play round it. In all its four avenues, each of which is made of red sandstone, and completed with a breadth of 20 gaz, there is a channel 6 gaz broad, which flows with 30 playing fountains in its centre. At the left and right (sides) of this garden two charming buildings (Sawan and Bhadon) decorated with pictures and paintings like the enamelled throne of the Queen of Shaiba, or like Solomon's throne studded with emeralds, have been built. Through the two water-ways of the tanks which are made in the centre of these buildings, the water is constantly bursting forth gracefully, and from the edge of their platforms, which have the height of 1½ gaz (from the ground), it falls into the tank below in the form of a cascade. In the niches, flower-vases of gold and silver, full of golden flowers, are placed during the daytime, and at night, white wax candles which appear like the stars in the thin clouds, are lighted and placed inside the veil of water.[11]

The last Mughal Emperor Bahadur Shah Zafar, built another pavilion in the centre of the main tank, named after him, Zafar Mahal. Originally there was a bridge to enter this pavilion, but it was destroyed soon after 1857.

The luxurious hammam or bath was also a noteworthy feature of most havelis. Built of marble, these shallow pools were fed with water drawn from wells, or through a tributary of the Nahar-i-Bihisht. The bath complex usually consisted of a minimum of three rooms: separate rooms for hot and cold baths, and a dressing room. Of course, there were variations. It is said that the hammams in Saadat

BELOW:
A du chhatti as it has survived in a haveli today.

OVERLEAF LEFT:
Terraces of the old city. The different levels on which they are built is an interesting feature.

OVERLEAF RIGHT:
Steps leading to a tehkhana. Few tehkhanas survive today, but in the past they were an essential feature of a haveli, providing an ideal retreat during the hot summer.

OPPOSITE PAGE:

The double walls forming the wind catching shaft.

The Bhadon pavilion (LEFT) in the Hayat Baksh garden in the Red Fort. The water-channel with fountains in it connected the Bhadon pavilion to the Savan pavilion at the other end. Between the two pavilions stands the Zafar Mahal (ABOVE).

Khan's haveli consisted of five rooms, covered with a glass dome. Once again the model for emulation was the royal bath in the Red Fort. Situated next to the Diwan-i-Khas, the hammam consisted of three main apartments, built of marble and inlaid with many coloured stones, both precious and semi-precious. Sir Syed Ahmed Khan writes:

The Hammam complex has been so marvellously planned and wrought that it has no comparison in the world. Its first part is a (spacious) room which is of marble up to the dados (including the pavement), bearing carved and inlaid designs. The eastern side is closed with jalies having glass pieces through which pleasant sceneries of the river-side and greenery are visible. The second part has on its northern side a Shah-Nashin (Seat of the Emperor) which is entirely built of carved and inlaid marble. A portion of it is square, also built of white marble, the whole having been profusely inlaid with coloured stones in floral designs. The ornamentation is wonderfully exquisite and it gives the impression of an Iranian carpet. . . .[12]

So much effort was invested in the construction of the more elaborate hammams that their utilization must have exceeded that of purely a 'bathroom'. There is evidence that the Mughal kings received very select visitors in the hammam, the rooms being used then as a more private extension of the Diwan-i-Khas. Several important court functions also were related to the *ghusul* or bath, such as that of the *ghusul-i-sehat*, when the monarch, after recovery from illness, participated in ceremonial ablutions. Certainly, the maintenance of the hammams was not an easy task. The job of keeping an assured and constant supply of fresh water and maintaining the vapour slabs, fountains, and drainage systems in good

The richly decorated hammam in the Red Fort. Elaborate hammams, patterned after the one in the Red Fort, were an integral part of the havelis too, but almost none are identifiable today.

repair, apart from the expense of heating the water, makes it quite obvious that the nawabs of Delhi were prepared to go to any length and incur considerable expense to live the way they felt they should. It is said that 125 maunds of wood were burnt on one day alone for the warm water operations in the Red Fort.

It has been recorded that when Shah Jahan entered the Red Fort for the first time, the entire roof, walls and colonnades of the Diwan-i-Aam were hung with velvet and silk from China and the furniture covered with rich cushions and Kashmiri shawls. This penchant for opulent interiors extended itself to the havelis. Bernier, the ever observant witness wrote:

At the most conspicuous side of the chamber are one or two mattresses, with fine coverings quilted in the form of flowers and ornamented with delicate silk embroidery, interspersed with gold and silver. These are intended for the master of the house, or any person of quality who may happen to call. Each mattress has a large cushion of brocade to lean upon, and there are other cushions placed round the room, covered with brocade, velvet of flowered satin, for the rest of the company. Five or six feet from the floor, the sides of the room are full of niches, cut in a variety of shapes, tasteful and well proportioned, in which are seen porcelain vases and flowerpots. The ceiling is gilt and painted. . . .[13]

Some of the large rooms had fire places; the smaller rooms were heated with *sigris*, full of red-hot coals. Tile work was much in evidence, most commonly seen up to a height of 5 to 6 ft from the floor. These ceramic tiles came in beautiful patterns. Windows, doors and roshandans were embellished with stained glass. Family portraits were the most acceptable form of wall adornment. Crystal chandeliers, of varying sizes, some very large indeed, were commonly found.

Bernier appraised the buildings of Delhi as a composite unit and recorded his own remarkably eclectic conclusion:

I think it may be safely asserted, without disparagement to the towns in our quarter of the globe, that the capital of Hindustan is not destitute of handsome buildings, although they bear no resemblance to those in Europe.[14]

From 1638 to the early years of the eighteenth century, the construction and expansion of havelis coincided with substantive political power vesting in the nobility, alongwith a sharp increase in its revenues from landed estates. The havelis of the leading members of the nobility

then approximated palace estates. Among the better known havelis were those of Ali Mardan Khan, Jafar Khan, Shaista Khan and Mahabat Khan. Those were the days of Shah Jahan and Aurangzeb. Mughal prestige and authority was still unquestioned, and despite the troubles that had begun to grow at the periphery of the empire, Delhi and its environs were still very much secure.

However, by the mid-eighteenth century, the Mughal Empire was in irreversible decline. Successive invaders—Afghans, Rohillas, Jats, Marathas—rampaged through Delhi and its neighbourhood. The erosion of central authority led to the breakdown of law and order; traditional 'criminal tribes' such as the Gujars to the north of Delhi, resumed their depredations with impunity. The environs of Delhi became unsafe and the descendants of those who had built their spacious estates in the suburbs, withdrew into the relative security of the walled city. A contemporary has recorded that by 1776 most of the suburban constructions had been reduced to rubble, overtaken once again by the wild beasts of the adjoining jungles. There was one other consequence of the decline of the Mughal rule: the power of some of the leading members of the nobility grew in direct proportion to the inexorable weakening of the king. Thus, while the condition of the imperial fortress haveli deteriorated pathetically, some omrahs, fattening on the opportunities of plunder and pillage that accompany such situations, grew in wealth and influence, their havelis reflecting this turn in the tide of fortune.

Safdarjung of Oudh was one such amir. In the 1750s, under the very nose of the now paralysed Mughal seat of power, he fought a civil war for the control of Delhi. His haveli, it is said, had several hundred rooms, with an ability to accommodate five thousand soldiers and five hundred horses. By contrast, Bishop Heber, who visited Delhi in 1825 and had an audience with the Mughal king, has recorded that in the Red Fort, the Naqqar Khana was 'ominous and exceedingly dirty'; the Diwan-i-Khas was 'dirty, desolate and forlorn', with old furniture piled in one corner, and a torn and faded tapestry hanging over the door which lead to the inner apartments;

and the Diwan-i-Aam was 'full of lumber of all descriptions, broken palanquins and empty boxes, . . . the throne so covered with pigeon's dung that its ornaments were hardly discernible'.[15] The good Bishop could not help writing that this could hardly be said to be the same palace which Bernier had seen and described two hundred years ago. 'The spider hangs her tapestry', he wrote philosophically, 'in the palace of the Caesars.'

This period of unceasing political turmoil settled to a 'frozen peace' when in 1803, after defeating the Marathas in battle, the British established *de facto* political power over the city. The Mughal king was still the *de jure* sovereign, but his writ did not extend beyond the ramparts of the fort, and his income had been reduced to that of a *mansabdar*. Except for the short-lived spurt in the wealth and power of a few members of the nobility during the period of political chaos coterminous with the decline of Mughal power, the amir-o-umara of Delhi were in general, by this time, a considerably more impoverished lot. However, even in the absence of earlier affluence, lifestyles, and consumption patterns continued to model themselves on the past, more often than not on credit made available by the merchant money-lender. The havelis were therefore maintained to the extent possible as before, although here and there, the paint and polish was showing signs of neglect.

In this initial colonial phase, there was no dramatic change: the basic urban profile persisted; some of the older havelis were, with certain modifications, taken over by the British, such as that of Ali Mardan which became the first British Residency. The British built mansions of their own, modelling them, in spite of the exteriors being different, upon the basic format of the haveli. Dr Ludlow, the Civil Surgeon, who had become a Delhiwallah through long years of stay, built Ludlow Castle, to the north outside Kashmiri Gate. Thomas Metcalfe, British Resident from 1835 to 1853, built the stately Metcalfe House along the river front. Sir Edward Colebrooke who took over the Residency in 1828, built his mansion on the Ridge. It was later bought by Hindu Rao, and the building that has survived today still has that name. Begum Samru built her haveli near Chandni

Peeling plaster amidst glimpses of a past grandeur.

Chowk, and the intrepid and colourful James Skinner constructed
his town house near Kashmiri Gate. Indeed, even though land-revenue,
the basic source of wealth of the umaras, had dwindled to a trickle
after the 1750s, Sir Syed Ahmed Khan's authoritative catalogue of
historical monuments and buildings, *Asar-us-Sanaadid*, as also the
chronicle maintained by the British, 'List of Hindu and Muhammadan
Monuments of Delhi', makes clear that construction activity, albeit
not on the same scale as a hundred years earlier, had far from
ceased.

Havelis, and an entire culture which was associated with them,
received their first grevious blow in 1857, the year Delhi, like other
parts of India, stood up in revolt against the British. When the British
recaptured the city, they were committed to ensure that the city
would never revolt again. This led to two basic developments: firstly,
large parts of the city were destroyed to make it more porous to the
rulers' gaze; secondly, the old feudal class was paupered beyond
redemption, its properties confiscated and auctioned off and its place
taken up, under active encouragement by the British, by a newly
aggressive *Lalocracy* (mercantile class).

Soon after the city was recaptured, there was a serious proposal
to demolish the Red Fort itself. While saner counsels ultimately prevented such a step, 80 per cent of the interior of the palace, occupy-
ing an area of 120 acres, was destroyed and replaced by military
barracks. In order to have a clear line of fire beyond the fort, all
buildings, within a radius of 448 yards from it, including the Urdu
Bazaar and Khas Bazaar, were razed to the ground. Initially, Dariba
too was to come under the purview of the demolition squad. But

ultimately it had a narrow escape. Havelis and localities that came in the way of the construction of two new boulevards—Queen's Road and Hamilton Road—were also destroyed. The construction of a railway line led to the removal of all buildings within the walled city in a 300 yard area running all the way from east to west. A third of the total walled area of the city was irretrievably altered for the creation of a cantonment. All of the above mutilation was in addition to the lethal damage which many havelis, and large parts of the city, had suffered from cannon fire during the siege of the city, and the battle for its recapture.

This wanton destruction was accompanied by one of the most remarkable revolutions in the ownership of urban property:

Extensive property belonging to those who had participated in the rebellion, or were suspected to have done so, had been confiscated by the British authorities. They now decided that those whose houses had been demolished could be compensated by allotments of similar value from this confiscated property. To implement the scheme, tickets indicating the value of the demolished property were given to the owners who could then exchange them for the new allotments. At first glance, it was a simple and ingenious scheme. But schemes such as these do not operate in an inert socio-economic milieu. The tickets were bought from the original assignees by a handful of rich merchants and bankers who, operating through an informal cartel, cornered vast properties at a time when the price of land was exceptionally low. The alternative British scheme, of auctioning confiscated property, also helped these very people, who in any case, had already appropriated considerable portions of it by claiming that the original occupants were their mortgagees. The entire operation thus acted as a catalyst for the organized emergency of a new mercantile class, and the further pauperization of the old feudal elite.[16]

Prize agents, officially given 'digging tickets' to search for treasure, put the final touches to this irremediable picture of desecration. Families stood and watched silently, as artefacts collected over decades—chandeliers and porcelain, gold and silver, carpets and furniture—were taken away as legal plunder.

In the period following the 1860s, the great havelis of Delhi either ceased to exist or stood as mute and forlorn witnesses to a past disrupted beyond repair. Nawabs, who had lived in the cloistered security of the family haveli, now found themselves evicted, or residents of the outhouses or even stables of their own mansions. Entire families of umara migrated from Delhi, leaving behind their family home to tenants or new owners. Nawab Azam Khan's mansion was bought by the Jutewala family; Bishamber Nath purchased the house of one of the sons of Shah Alam II; Pandit Jwalanath took over the haveli of Nawab Muzaffar Khan, and Hardhyan Singh occupied Haveli Hamid Ali Khan; Sir Syed Ahmed Khan's houses became the property of one Sheikh Nasir Ali. Ghalib wrote: 'Helplessly, I watch the wives and children of aristrocrats actually begging from door to door. One must have a heart of steel to witness the contemporary scene.'

Havelis cannot be studied merely in terms of brick and mortar, as architectural curiosities, unaffected by the ebb and flow of historical change around them. They cannot be seen in isolation from the city of which they were a part. Their *raison d'etre* was interwoven with a pace and a rhythm which pervaded Shahjahanabad as a whole; this relationship was so inherent that the tampering with any

The past and the present— artistry of a different kind.

OVERLEAF:

Fading memories of another age. Carved stone columns along one of the galis of Shahjahanabad. The carving on the extreme right depicts a hunting scene.

one aspect of the city, would have an unavoidable effect on all the constituents that combined to give it its unmistakable profile. In the ultimate analysis, therefore, the decline of the haveli was linked to the decline of Shahjahanabad itself.

Havelis flourished in Shahjahanabad because it came to provide an unparalleled 'residential' environment. In the period after 1857, many facets of such an environment began to be relentlessly eroded. The somewhat thoughtless construction of the railway line in 1860, right through the prime residential area within the city, started the process. Gradually the city became more and more commercialized. The extension of the railway line in the 1890s to the south-west, just outside the walled city, and the introduction of electricity in 1902, gave a fillip to this inexorable trend. The remnants of the feudal elite had not the wherewithal to resist this pressure. Indeed, with dwindling or non-existent sources of income, they welcomed developments which allowed them to rent out part of their havelis to mechanized workshops, or to warehouses. In 1885, the city had ten *karkhanas*; two decades later there were several flour and saw mills, and innumerable factory establishments.

A karigar in the walled city displaying the varak (silver foil) painstakingly made by him. Such craftsmanship has changed little since the days of Shah Jahan.

When in 1911, it was decided to shift the British capital to Delhi, both Lutyens and Baker initially wanted to integrate the old city with the new in a manner that would allow the former to retain its essential character and yet stem the chaotic commercialization and industrialization that was destroying it. 'A long processional avenue was planned from the fort through Delhi Gate, past a park and a boulevard with the houses of Indian princes lining both sides. Another was to cut through the side of the Jama Masjid from the proposed King Edward Memorial Park, and bear south-westward to the new railway station, whence another road was to lead to Kashmiri Gate.' These roads were never built. Thus it was that the sharp contrast between an expansive residential area and an over-congested commercial slum was formalized and perpetuated.

In 1916, another opportunity presented itself, when the government, after a detailed survey published a listing of Muslim and Hindu buildings of architectural importance in the walled city. However, the opportunity was lost because for some inexplicable reason almost all the listed monuments were placed in the category where no preservation measures were recommended. 'Thus a study that might have been the first step toward preserving the architectural fabric of old Delhi became almost detrimental in this regard. Anyone consulting the list would have received assurance that old Delhi had been thoroughly examined and judged largely unworthy of protective efforts.'[17]

Today, the walled city has become a major grain market; it is also the centre of a huge publishing industry; its mohallas and kuchas house wholesale stockists of iron pipes, paints, chemicals, automobile parts, heavy machinery, construction materials and electronic components. Small factories run lathes in its narrowest galis. The congestion is so great that one can barely walk on even its broadest streets. Gone are the gracious environs, canals and gardens, the quiet residential mohallas. A Town Hall has replaced Jahanara's Serai. The Nahar-i-Bihisht has dried up; cement and concrete covers the beautiful tree-lined canal that flowed through the Chandni Chowk. The luxurious tehkhanas have been sealed, since the abandonment

and neglect of walls in recent times led to a rise in the water table, causing seepage and flooding. Even today there are residents who recall that up to the 1940s there were areas in the city, so quiet, that the 'tuk . . . tuk . . . tuk' sound of the *karigar* (artisan) beating silver and gold into *varak* (thin foils) could be heard clearly within a radius of a furlong.

Not too long ago, during the summer months, at about five in the evening when the worst heat of the day was on the wane, a bullock cart laden with water would start its leisurely, water sprinkling journey from the Town Hall, passing by the Fountain, Chandni Chowk, Jama Masjid, Chawri Bazaar, Hauz Qazi and other important areas. The route taken was known as the *Thandi Sarak* or Cool Street. The entire city would awake around this time, from its afternoon siesta. Today, innumerable industrial establishments work through the night, be it summer or winter. Generations of successive partitions between heirs and collaterals have reduced the havelis into multi-tenant hovels. In truth, the havelis are no more because the Shahjahanabad that sustained them is no more.

The elite of Shahjahanabad has left for the newly emergent 'colonies' of New Delhi. For some who have stayed, there is often a sense of bewilderment about what to do with a home that can no longer be maintained. Neglect and desuetude are constant companions of rooms and roofs, courtyards, pillars and arches. A few have converted their havelis to guest houses. But in their so doing, the haveli is hardly recognizable. Its many noble features have been summarily done away with to create a new, more 'functional' structure. The shabby transformation is so complete that one has to be reminded that once, not so long ago, another building of another age and another design stood here.

What is even more distressing is the conscious repudiation of a heritage, the denial of a legacy, by its natural heirs and inheritors. Those who have moved away from Shahjahanabad but still need to visit it daily, because their shop or warehouse or workshop is located there, have chosen to consciously live at dual levels of identity. When in the walled city, they allow themselves to lapse into the

The mouth-watering enticements of Shahjahanabad.

Some elements of the lifestyle of the past still persist–kabutar bazi in the walled city.

cultural *lehza* (idiom) of the place, including its sartorial requirements, such as a dhoti kurta, essential when you are to be seated on a *gaddi* (thin mattress) supported by the familiar *masnat* or *gao takiya* (bolster pillows). At the end of the day, they change into a safari suit and recede purposefully into the aggressive if nondescript socio-cultural mainstream of the newer city. The culture of New Delhi has the aura of success and money. The ambience of Shahjahanabad has an unmistakable melancholy, the odour of a past that cannot be resurrected any more; it is a profile tinged with sadness, reminiscent of a courtesan past her salad days, unable to find patrons any more.

The children of those who had lived in the havelis till not so far back, the new generation, will know little about the culture, the way of life, that has been left behind. Their parents, however, still have a lurking nostalgia for the authentic milieu of which they were once a part. The call of the kuchas and mohallas, where life unfolded amidst familiar landmarks underpinned by centuries of tradition, remains strong. This is the unambiguous impression I have after talking to many a former haveliwallah. There reminiscences are not merely intense; they transparently articulate a regret.

It was not for nothing that Zauq, the poet and tutor of the last Mughal King Bahadur Shah Zafar, had proclaimed: '*Kaun jaye par ab, Dilli ki galiyan chhod kar*' (who can, after all, leave the streets of Delhi). After the destruction of 1857, an entire body of poetry—*Shahr-i-Ashob*—emerged to lament the destruction of Delhi and the gracious way of life it nurtured. Today, those who live in Shahjahanabad, are still sometimes awakened by the call of the itinerant vendors, selling their wares in the same rhythmic, sing-song voice

that resounded in these alleys and byways a hundred years ago. At the crack of dawn, the aroma of mouth-watering *nihari*, nurturing a culinary secret generations old, will still not fail to entice. On an evening, a visitor to the city will still see *kabutar baz* on the roof-tops flying pigeons with infectious enthusiasm. A few buildings, very few indeed, still have 'those mysterious upper storeys, with their wooden balconies, their reticent lattices, their dim alluring mysteries, where are glimpses of vague figures with gleaming armlets and shining necklaces, telling of an unwritten aspect of many sided Delhi'.[18] A few landmarks can still be seen to hold their sway, unaffected by time and change. But, for the greater part, Shahjahanabad has lost most of what prompted Sir Syed Ahmed Khan to assert:

Kasra zindgani shad bashad ki dar Shah-e-jahan abad bashad

The man who fortunately finds residence in the city of Shahjahanabad, leads a happy life.

NOTES

1 Francois Bernier, *Travels in the Mogul Empire*, rpt., Delhi, 1989, p. 241.
2 Ibid., p. 243.
3 Ibid., p. 245.
4 Stephen P. Blake, 'Cityscape of an Imperial Capital: Shahjahanabad in 1739', in R. E. Frykenberg (ed.), *Delhi through the Ages*, Delhi, 1986, p. 160.
5 Sir Syed Ahmed Khan, *Asar-us-Sanaadid*, trans. R. Nath, *Monuments of Delhi*, New Delhi, 1979.
6 *Gazetteer of Delhi District* (1883–4), rpt., Delhi, 1988, p. 42.
7 Francois Bernier, *Travels*, p. 240.
8 Major Archer, *Travels in Northern India*, vol. I, London, 1833, p. 108.
9 Francois Bernier, *Travels*, p. 247.
10 Satish Grover, 'The Islamic Influence in Architecture', in *Muslims in India*, New Delhi, 1990.
11 Muhammad Salih Lahori, *Amal-i-Salih*, mss, Lahore, folios 580-2.
12 Sir Syed Ahmed Khan.
13 Francois Bernier, *Travels*, p. 248.
14 Ibid., p. 248.
15 Quoted in M. A. Laird (ed.), *Bishop Heber in Northern India*, Cambridge, 1971, p. 235.
16 Pavan K. Varma, *Ghalib, the Man, the Times*, New Delhi, 1989, p. 167.
17 Norma Everson, *The Indian Metropolis*, Delhi, 1969.
18 Lovat Fraser, *At Delhi*, London, 1903.

Chunna Mal's Haveli

غافل بہ وہم ناز خود آرا ہے، ورنہ یاں

بے شانۂ صبا نہیں طُرّہ گیاہ کا

Confused, full of its own importance,
the ego itself depicts,
But unless the wind caresses it,
a weed is not a whip.

Ghalib

CHUNNA MAL'S HAVELI is situated at the point where Katra Nil, a narrow but important gali, meets Chandni Chowk. Its frontage, covering an entire block, is on Chandni Chowk. Its western side is defined by Katra Nil.

Chunna Mal's forefathers had migrated to Delhi from Lahore around the end of the sixteenth century. In time they built up a flourishing business in shawls, brocades and textiles. These goods, the family claims, were supplied regularly to the Tosha Khanas (treasury) of the Mughal emperors. The family firm had branches in Calcutta and Farrukhabad as well. An important off-shoot of the hereditary business was money lending. Mirza Fakhru, the son and heir-apparent of the last Mughal King Bahadur Shah Zafar, was indebted to Chunna Mal. Apparently, he had borrowed more than he could pay back. Chunna Mal who had become rich by being strict with his debtors, obtained an order from the British Magistrate empowering him to seize Mirza Fakhru's assets. But the Mughal prince had a trump card up his sleeve. He quickly moved all his possessions to the Red Fort, where the royal family enjoyed immunity.

Chunna Mal's real moment of opportunity came in 1857. During the months of the Revolt (May to September 1857), when the British had been expelled from the city, Chunna Mal (so the family history claims) 'set a high standard of active loyalty . . . at a time when the slightest lurking partiality for the British, if discovered, meant death at the hands of the blood thirsty mutineers'. As events turned out, this demonstration of 'loyalty' paid rich dividends. The victorious British were in search of new 'native' allies. They actively encouraged the replacement of the old feudal elite by a new *Lalocracy*. Chunna Mal was the principal beneficiary of such a policy.

The aftermath of 1857 witnessed a revolution in the ownership of property in Delhi. For those who had the money and were in the good books of the British, this was the moment to buy land and buildings at ridiculously cheap prices. Chunna Mal had the money and the backing of the British. In a bizarre exercise in acquisition he bought over a great portion of Chandni Chowk, much of the pro-

ABOVE:

Lala Chunna Mal.

BELOW LEFT:

Lala Chunna Mal seated second from right.

perty in the city, vast tracts of suburban land and most of the crown jewels. Fatehpuri Mosque was also bought by him in 1860 for a little over Rs 39,000. It remained his private property until 1877, when Lord Lytton restored it to the Muslims. Four villages were given to Chunna Mal in return.

Chunna Mal's haveli had suffered little damage during the turbulent days of 1857. It was away from the city walls, and hence safe from the British shelling of the city from the Ridge. After they recaptured the city, Katra Nil, reputed to be one of the richest areas, was spared the looting and plunder unleashed by the British because it had paid 'ransom money'. As Chunna Mal's wealth and importance increased dramatically, his haveli became a landmark in the city, with the rich and influential queueing up to meet him. On festive occasions, such as Diwali, he would hold court for the rais and amirs of the city, his haveli lit up with chandeliers and candelabra. In one of his letters Ghalib has remarked that while the rest of Delhi was plunged in grief and darkness, Chunna Mal's haveli was so flooded with light that it made night look like day.

In 1862, when the first Municipality was formed, Chunna Mal was appointed a Municipal Commissioner. In 1864, the British made him the Honorary Magistrate of Delhi. Earlier, he had been given a *khillut* (high testimonial) and elevated to a Rai Bahadur. Chunna Mal had given enough evidence of his loyal activism to merit these honours. His record of public charity was impressive. The Municipality was largely financed by a huge loan given by him at a very low interest rate. He was one of the founders of the Anglo-Sanskrit School. His contributions to famine relief and public works were

A festive occasion in the haveli in happier times.

exceptionally generous. Of course his income could sustain such benevolence. In 1869, he was one of two Indians in Delhi whose recorded income was more than one lakh rupees a year.

The frontage of the haveli on Chandni Chowk.

Chunna Mal died in January 1870. After him, a succession of capable men—his nephew Umrao Singh (1869–79), Ram Kishen Das (1879–1902) and Sheo Parshad (1902–21)—kept up the commercial and social primacy of the family, always, of course, under the care of British patronage. Several more titles came the family's way. The Chunna Mal haveli continued playing a pivotal role in the life of Shahjahanabad. Its proximity to the newly built railway station (1868), the retail business of Chandni Chowk and the Town Hall (the new seat of local government) buttressed the prominence it enjoyed.

In some ways the haveli even functioned as an informal extension of the local administrative headquarters, with successive British Commissioners seeking the advice of the head of the Chunna Mal clan on issues such as relief works, compensation, educational policy, municipal affairs, and 'that most cordially obnoxious of measures the Income Tax . . .'. The family also used to assist the British in ensuring communal harmony during festivals such as Id and Dussehra, or when different communities simultaneously took out religious processions through the city—a potentially dangerous event. In 1886, the haveli was attacked during clashes between Ram Lila and Tazia processionists.

In 1877, Umrao Singh had installed some telephone instruments in the haveli 'which attracted crowds of wondering admirers'. He had also built a functional model of a railway engine large enough for a child to sit in, which was preserved till recently by his descen-

One of the rooms inside the haveli (ABOVE) and a surviving member of the family posing for a portrait by the side of an ornately decorated fire-place (BELOW).

dants. His successor, Ram Kishen Das was the founder, Managing Director and the largest share holder of the Delhi Cloth & General Mills Co. Ltd. It is said that the father of Lala Shri Ram, noted entrepreneur and industrialist, once worked in the haveli as a *munim* (clerk). The first car in the city was bought by the Chunna Mal family. For quite some time the car was parked outside the entrance of the haveli, attracting hordes of dazzled crowds and further enhancing the urban folk lore of the family's affluence. From the stables, the Deputy Commissioner regularly borrowed carriages and horses whenever a distinguished visitor came to Delhi.

In 1912, Lord Hardinge, the Viceroy of India, and Lady Hardinge arrived at the Delhi railway station, to formally take up residence in the new capital of India. They were to be taken from the station in a formal procession on elephant back, past the Town Hall and through Chandni Chowk to the Red Fort. During the procession, a bomb was hurled at the viceroy, grieviously wounding him and killing his *chaprasi* (peon). Lala Sheo Pershad, then head of the Chunna Mal family, spent Rs 200 to organize a *havan* (religious ceremony) for the recovery of H.E. the viceroy; he also gave Rs 500 to the family of the chaprasi.

Ram Parshad (1951–65) was the family's last *karta* or head. Today, three-fourths of the haveli is unoccupied. The remaining rooms are occupied by such descendants as have lingered on. Much of the riches of the haveli—chandeliers and furniture—have been cannibalized. One branch of the family stays in what was earlier the formal dining-room. This room alone has half a dozen chandeliers. The formal drawing-room is kept locked. The ground floor has been

OPPOSITE:

Some of the chandeliers remain though the lights have lost their lustre.

BELOW:

The steps leading up to the haveli.

RIGHT:

The family appears to have had a particular weakness for mirrors.

rented out to shops and is a wholesale cloth market. To create maximum area for the shops a main hall, from whose high ceilings hung dozens of chandeliers on ceremonial occasions, has been roofed at a lower level. Iron hooks, meant to hold the chandeliers, hang forlornly and meaninglessly from the original roof. There are 139 tenants, yielding a monthly income of only Rs 12,000. The stables at the back of the haveli, near Bagh Diwar, have been rented to the Amritsar Transport Company. Some property—the Majestic and Jubilee cinemas, shops opposite Gurudwara Sis Ganj—remains with the joint family. Most of the remaining property has long been partitioned and sold. The Swiss Hotel in Civil Lines was bought by the Oberois in 1968. Ludlow Castle was acquired by the government and converted into a school. Gulabi Bagh near Roshanara Club, which measured 24 acres, was also acquired by the government. Ram Bagh, which had a swimming pool and a mini-zoo, was sold in 1950 for a paltry sum of four lakh rupees.

A large clock, overlooking Chandni Chowk, adorns the frontage
of Chunna Mal's haveli. The clock has not functioned for decades.
Nothing, indeed, could be more symbolic of the state of the havelis
today.

Haveli Begum Samru

اس کے پیچھے چھپی ہیں کتنی دیواریں
جسم کی یہ دیوار گرا کے دیکھوں گا

The wall of the body
I will demolish, to find
How many more walls remain
Hidden behind.

Anas Moim

O̲N̲ CHANDNI CHOWK, if you turn right at Kumar Talkies, and walk a few yards on, you will come to an imposing mansion, whose classic collonaded features are hardly visible anymore under the onslaught of display boards of several hundred shops selling electrical goods. The building, which is today known as Bhagirath Place, and has become Delhi's premier electrical mart, was the cherished haveli of one of Delhi's most colourful personalities in the last century—Begum Samru.

Begum Samru was born in the 1750s. Her origins are obscure. According to some, she is supposed to have hailed from a good Mughal family; others maintain that she was a Muslim of common stock from Kashmir. When still very young, she was married (some say, sold as a slave) to a French mercenary, Walter Reinhardt. Reinhardt's career graph was typical of a great number of men of European origin who, in the politically turbulent and fractured landscape of India in the seventeenth century, made their living as soldiers on hire. Reinhardt, on arrival in India, had joined a Swiss corps in Calcutta which he deserted in fifteen days. He then fled to U.P. and served under Safdarjung. Soon thereafter he left Safdarjung and joined the forces of the nawab of Bengal. He died in 1776, but by then had acquired a large fortune, and a lucrative principality with its capital at Sardana in Meerut. His wealth and estates were inherited by Begum Samru.

The Begum's name, Samru, has a very interesting origin. Walter Reinhardt had assumed the name Summer, 'but from the darkness of his complexion he received the sobriquet "Sombre", subsequently corrupted into Sumroo, by which name Her Highness was generally known, though she always styled herself the Begum Sombre'. The Begum was of a diminutive stature and of fair complexion. On succeeding to the principality of her husband she showed leadership and administrative skills of uncommon quality. Her *jagir* yielded an annual income of close to ten lakh rupees a year. She headed a disciplined and large body of troops which she often led into battle

TOP:

Begum Samru.

MIDDLE:

The Begum with her paramour.

BELOW:

The tumult of 1857 left many scars on the haveli.

Begum Samru's haveli at Sardana, the seat of her vast estates, which served as a model for her haveli at Delhi.

herself. Before the establishment of British rule in Delhi, she was aligned with the Marathas who were in *de facto* control of the city. Her relations with the Mughal Emperor Shah Alam II were excellent. He referred to her as his 'most beloved daughter', an appellation she was shrewd enough to have engraved on her personal seal. Once it became apparent that the British forces would defeat the Marathas, the Begum, in an agile diplomatic move, transferred her loyalties to the former. In 1803, when Lord Lake defeated the Marathas at the battle of Patparganj, near Delhi, the Begum's troops were on the winning side. The British, grateful for her support, granted her several more jagirs and awarded her recognition as an independent ruler.

For several decades, Kothi Begum Samru was a landmark of considerable importance in Shahjahanabad. It is difficult to imagine this now, but in those days, the mansion stood in imposing aloofness in the midst of a huge and tastefully laid out garden estate, extending from the present Kumar Talkies in the south to Mor Serai in the north (the haveli's stables were located at this end), and from the Fountain in the west to beyond the existing Lala Lajpat Rai Market in the east. From Chandni Chowk, a long cypress-lined drive led to the haveli.

The Begum, who always dressed in Indian costumes of the most costly material, had the reputation of being a hostess of impeccable repute. Soon after the death of her husband she had converted to Christianity.[1] This factor, in addition to her support for the British, made her lavish dinners quite acceptable to the *Angrez Bahadur*

(English officers). Lord Lake, the conqueror of Patparganj, frequently supped with her. His successors continued the practice. The Begum did not speak English, but aided by an interpreter, presided over her sit-down banquets with great verve and equanimity. The following is a contemporary's account of a dinner at her haveli:

At the Begum Sumroo's palace we found thirty persons of rank assembled, and a splendid banquet in the European style. This ended, she arose and threw over the shoulders of each of the ladies a wreath of flowers formed of a tuberose plant, united by narrow gold ribbon. No sooner was she re-seated, then strains of soft music were heard, and two folding doors of the saloon flew open as if by enchantment, discovering a number of young girls in the attitude of dancing a ballet, or, as it is here termed, a 'notch'.[2]

The Begum's personality made her haveli quite a symbol of romantic passion and intrigue. In 1787, some ten years after her husband's death, her Commander-in-Chief, George Thomas (a mercenary briefly in her employ, who carved out a principality for himself in Hansi) caught her eye. The Begum was still young, in her thirties, and the affair blossomed quickly. The general expectation was that the two would get married but, just then, a younger man, this time a French mercenary called Le Vessoult took her fancy. The two eloped, an act which provoked even her otherwise disciplined troops to revolt. Le Vessoult was captured and committed suicide. Begum Samru, attempted suicide, survived, and ultimately regained the confidence of her men.

She died in 1837 at the age of 85. Her adopted son, by the name of David Ochterlony Dyce Sombre,[3] succeeded to her haveli. Dyce

The rear facade of the haveli.

left India for England in 1842, where he assumed the status of 'some celebrity', having married the daughter of Lord St. Vincent. One of the Begum's daughters married an Englishman, and the other, an Italian Baron. In 1847, Dyce sold the haveli to the newly formed Delhi Bank. Prior to this, there was a move to house the Kacheri (Law Courts) in the building, since the Kotwali (Police Station) on Chandni Chowk was so close by, but the Bank, supported by men like Lala Chunna Mal, and a large body of Hindu, Muslim and European subscribers, was able to raise sufficient capital to lay the first claim.

The Delhi Bank formally started commercial transaction in 1850. A part of the mansion was the residence of the Bank's Manager, Mr Beresford, an Englishman. In May 1857, when the Great Revolt broke, the troopers attacked Beresford. One of the most dramatic events in the history of the haveli took place then. Beresford fought his attackers with courage, but was driven to the roof of the house, where, grossly outnumbered, he was killed. His wife and children met the same fate. It is said that Mrs Beresford killed two of her attackers with a hog-spear before she was killed herself.

In 1859, the Delhi Bank recommenced its operations at the haveli. From then onwards the building was associated with banking—with the Imperial Bank, and later the Lloyds Bank as its tenant—until 1922, when Munshi Shiv Narain purchased it. It was from Shiv Narain that Lala Bhagirath Mal bought it in 1940. Shiv Narain had taken a loan from Lloyds Bank and mortgaged the haveli to it. When he was unable to repay the loan, Bhagirath Mal bought

67

the building. With the surplus money he acquired through the sale, Shiv Narain bought a house on Rajpur Road.

Lala Bhagirath Mal's ancestors were in the *gota-kinari* (gold thread) trade. His father, Bishambernath, had gone into wholesale cloth business, and with it gained prosperity. Bhagirath Mal was the second man in Delhi to buy a car (it was a 1936 Fiat; the first car was bought by the Chunna Mal family). Bhagirath Mal did not live in the main haveli, but in a twenty-five room outhouse within the garden compound (Bagh Begum Samru) of the haveli. The present owner, Amarnath Gupta, Bhagirath Mal's son, recalls the abundance of fruit trees in the vast compound—mango, date, jamun, lukat, anjir. There were then no buildings in the area between the haveli and the Red Fort. The present Lala Lajpat Rai Market was a football field. In the evening, Bhagirath Mal would often take a ride in his phaeton with his family. On reaching the edge of Edward Park near Darya Ganj, he would urge the *saees* to turn back for fear of being robbed. The main haveli, although unoccupied, was maintained in good condition and often rented out to marriage parties, its many large halls making it a favourite venue. Amarnath Gupta recalls a large hall at the back of the building with exquisite parquet flooring, probably used as a dance floor in times gone by. In the basement of the building, marble baths could be seen till very recently. Amarnath Gupta also recalls a tunnel which the family had closed.

The baths have now been occupied by a maze of shops. The garden estate no longer exists. In 1959, the family built a hotel on the portion where there was a huge well and a hammam complex. For all the changes, amazingly, the faint letterings in bold capital—

The haveli, or what remains of it, today. Behind the hoarding on top, the fading letters of Lloyds Bank can still be seen.

Begum Samru's Church off
Chandni Chowk.

LLOYDS BANK—can still be seen on the building's frontage. The
past persists in the basic structure of the building—its classic columns,
and the green wooden *jaffri* in the verandah. Perhaps, after dusk,
when all the shops have closed and the city is asleep, the columns
recall the era when Begum Samru, resplendently dressed in the
choicest silks, stood in the verandah at the top of the staircase to
welcome her guests, and one could hear the crunch of gravel as
elegant horse carriages came down the long cypress-lined driveway.

NOTES

1. She built a church near her haveli which can still be seen on Chandni
   Chowk.
2. A. Deare, *A Tour through the Upper Provinces of Hindustan*, London, 1823,
   quoted in H. K. Kaul (ed.), *Historic Delhi*, Delhi, 1985.
3. This was the name of Delhi's first British Resident in 1804. The Begum had
   given his name to her adopted son in an obvious attempt to please the
   Resident.

Namak Haram ki Haveli

بے دَر و دیوار کا اک گھر بنایا چاہیے
کوئی ہمسایہ نہ ہو اور پاسباں کوئی نہ ہو

Build a house sans walls or floor
No neighbour, no person, close-by should be.

Ghalib

If you are walking on Chandni Chowk, away from the Red Fort, there is towards the end of the street, when you have almost reached Fatehpuri Masjid, a narrow gali to your right, leading into Kucha Ghasi Ram. Flanking the entrance to this kucha is a fruit juice shop, and a *mithai* shop doing brisk business. Wending your way along Kucha Ghasi Ram, you will pass under an arched gateway and enter Chhatta Bhowani Shankar. Bhowani Shankar built Namak Haram ki haveli almost two centuries ago. Portions of this noble mansion stand even today, although in inconsolable ruin.

There is historical reason why this haveli was given such a disparaging name. Bhowani Shankar was born in Delhi towards the end of the seventeenth century. Restless by disposition, he left Delhi, when still young, to join the rebel Maratha leader Jaswant Rao Holkar. Bhowani served Jaswant Rao with exceptional loyalty and courage throughout the many years of his implacable battle with the rival Maratha line of the Scindias. In one of the battles, where Scindia inflicted a crushing defeat on Jaswant Rao's forces, Bhowani Shankar

LEFT:
The main entrance to the haveli.

BELOW:
A detail depicting the floral pattern on the arch.

OPPOSITE:
A beautifully carved wooden doorway and an arch, part of the original haveli complex.

Electric wires weave their own pattern on the haveli gateway (LEFT:), and (BELOW): glimpses of the exquisite carvings that still survive.

lost the fingers on his hand due to bayonet injuries. However, in 1803, when the British and the Maratha armies prepared to clash in the decisive battle of Patparganj, near Delhi, Bhowani Shankar deserted Jaswant Rao and defected to the British. In fairness, it must be said that petty intrigue and favouritism in Jaswant Rao's camp had made Bhowani Shankar's position very difficult. However, for the common man, this act of treachery from a person from whom it was expected the least, was unpardonable. The British rewarded Bhowani Shankar by giving him high office. Bhowani Shankar was also a rich man in his own right. The haveli he built for himself in the city of his birth was one of considerable opulence and luxury. For the people of Delhi it remained nevertheless, 'Namak Haram ki haveli'.

Bhowani Shankar's descendants fell on difficult days. His son Jai Singh, who died in 1862, was forced to mortgage his ancestral haveli. It is likely that when the Revolt of 1857 erupted, Namak Haram ki haveli was occupied by its new owners. Many inhabitants of Kucha Ghasi Ram believe that the unusual name of the mansion has something to do with the events of 1857. According to this less authentic lore, the owner of the haveli in 1857, a prominent Muslim, was forced to flee from Delhi when the British recaptured the city. He left the haveli and all his possessions therein in the safe-keeping of a servant. Much later, after the tumult of 1857 had ebbed, the owner returned only to find that the servant he had trusted was a *namak haram*. He had usurped the title to the mansion.

It is almost impossible to picture this now, but the haveli, as originally built, was a beautiful complex of gardens, pavilions and waterways. Near the main haveli, whose imposing but ruinously desolate gateway still stands, was Bhowani Shankar's kacheri or court building. A large *baoli* or stepped-well, built entirely of marble was located opposite the mansion. It had a separate section demarcated by marble screens for the ladies. The baoli was mercilessly demolished as recently as 1973. A few public spirited local inhabitants complained to the authorities to prevent the desecration, to no avail. The well was so rich that water continued seeping out even after it was closed. A thicker concrete slab was then slapped over it. The baoli is now

LEFT:

A fountain which no longer
works, but which once graced
Bhowani Shankar's garden.

an underground godown for spices and condiments. Even today, if
you step into the godown, you will feel a cool draft, for the temperature
remains several degrees lower than outside. Some local inhabitants
still recall that the father of the present owner of the haveli used to
sit at the baoli, dipping a hook attached to a long string into the
well. He was searching for treasure, for it was said that, in 1857,
when the owner of the haveli was fleeing for his life, he had thrown
the family jewels into the baoli.

To the west of the haveli was Bhowani Shankar's baradari, set in
a small but exquisite garden with several fountains. At least one of
these fountains can still be seen in the courtyard of an adjacent
house. To the east, at the entrance of the erstwhile haveli complex,
were the *astabals* (stables). Old local residents recall that a huge banyan tree shaded the entire area of the stables. The main haveli had
a magnificent tehkhana. This was inadvertently discovered some

The building once housed
Bhowani Shankar's stables.

time ago, when, due to the flooding caused by heavy rains, the floor
of one of the rooms caved in.

Today, Bhowani Shankar's baradari is an ugly, grey cement room.
The fountains have been uprooted. The waterways have been paved
over. The stables are a timber godown. The stone gateway, intricately carved, stands dirty and crumbling. The haveli has become a
multi-tenant hovel and here and there, amidst the clutter of new
construction, mostly illegal, one can see glimpses of the old architectural edifice. The present owner of the haveli does not know when
and how his family came into its ownership. He is vague in his
belief that it must have been sometime around the tumultuous days
of 1857, when a great deal of property changed hands. His main
concern is that he has ninety tenants who collectively yield a monthly
income of Rs 2400.

The present residents of the Namak Haram ki haveli complex
peg the continuing historical importance of their locality to the fact
that the legendary freedom fighter Bhagat Singh took refuge there
from the police, and that the Ramjas Foundations opened their first
school in Delhi in their kucha. A considerable section of the area is
a wholesale market for flowers, and is called Phool Walon ki Mandi.
Bhowani Shankar's garden is no more, but almost as if in tribute,
stacked in a room which must have been a part of the original
garden, are huge sacks of rose petals and gendas. The fragrance is
there but an unsettling melancholia sits heavily.

Zeenat Mahal

دل عشق میں ہمیشہ حریفِ نبرد تھا
اب جس جگہ کہ داغ ہے یاں پہلے درد تھا

In love, the heart was always concerned
About the rival's gain,
This spot where but a stain remains
One day pulsated with joy and pain.

Sir Syed Ahmed Khan

ZEENAT MAHAL BEGUM was the favourite queen of Bahadur Shah Zafar, the last Mughal King (1837–57). She lived in the Red Fort, but had her own haveli in the city. The haveli, named after her, Zeenat Mahal, is on the Lal Kuan Street, not far from Fatehpuri Masjid.

The entrance to the haveli is through a double arch made of red sandstone. The outer arch frames huge iron-studded wooden gates through which the queen used to enter in a covered palanquin, atop an elephant. Traditional drummers (*naqqarawallahs*) used to lead the royal procession; for this reason, local inhabitants used to call her *Danka* (colloquialism for drums) Begum. The height of the gate was reduced some decades ago, when the street outside was metalled and its level rose. Two beautiful *jharokha* (balcony) pavilions in red sandstone flank the gateway on top. A small marble plaque is embedded in the centre of the edifice. Engraved on it, in Persian, are the following words:

Kardaye Zafar Zeenat Mahal taamir-e-qasr bi badal
Shod bar mahal saal banaye khanah-e-Zeenat Mahal.

The work of Zafar,[1] an unmatched edifice, Zeenat Mahal.
This year commenced the construction of a house for Zeenat Mahal.

The marble plaque can hardly be seen today. A tattered canvas awning over a *halwai* (sweetmeat) shop outside the gateway partially covers it. Even if the plaque were visible, the engraving on it, under layers of dust and filth, is almost unreadable. A small banyan tree grows from one of the crevices of the pavilion. On the imposing wooden gate, a tin signboard announces the offices of the youth wing of the Congress party. An improvised *chai ka dhaba* (tea stall) uses the gate as a support. As you walk in, an electronic cacophony leads you to a busy video games parlour. A nursery school has taken over the rooms on the first floor. 'Shining Nursery School' reads a placard hanging lopsidedly from a window.

There are few havelis which have seen as much definitive desecration as the Zeenat Mahal haveli. Apart from the main gateway complex just described, hardly anything remains of what once was. However, the basic structure existed till the 1950s, and there are some old residents who vividly recall the details. It seems the gateway

opened into a courtyard ringed by a series of rooms with carved pillars supporting red sandstone arches. One desolate remnant of this structure has survived. These rooms opened further inwards into an intermediate courtyard paved with marble and in the centre of which stood a marble fountain. The innermost secluded area, beyond the courtyard, was in the nature of a large pavilion. Fourteen arches on the four sides opened inwards into the daalan and dar daalan familiar to all havelis. Marble courtyards surrounded the pavilion on all sides. Shade giving trees were planted at various places. There was a large and beautifully appointed tehkhana below the mansion. Local residents also remember with certainty, that two underground tunnels led off from the haveli, one in the direction of the Red Fort, and the other towards Ajmeri Gate. They can point precisely to the two spots from where the tunnels began. A third building—Nagina Mahal (Jewelled Palace)—stood at the back of this inner and central pavilion. A subsidiary entrance to the entire haveli complex was from the Farash Khana side on the south.

Zeenat Mahal haveli provided an appropriate setting for the personality of its owner. Though the Mughal empire had disintegrated and with it, the writ of her husband, the Begum was both tenacious and ambitious in pursuing her own agenda of action. Her hold over the king was considerable. Much younger than him, she was pretty, with finely chiselled features and the aging king, a poet, was quite capable of romantic infatuation. Perhaps it was when he met Zeenat for the first time that he wrote the lines:

ABOVE:
The frontage of the haveli today.

BELOW:
A close-up of the ceiling of the vestibule just inside the main gateway.

80

The past in a losing battle against
the encroaching shoddiness of
the present.

Le gaya loot ke kaun mera sabr-o-karar
Beqarari tujhe ai dil, kabhi aisi to na thi

Who is this who has looted my calm and restraint.
Such restlessness, my heart, has never obtained.

Soon after marriage, Zeenat Mahal Begum was blessed with a
son, Jiwan Bakht. From then onwards her over-riding ambition was
to ensure that her son succeed her husband to the throne, supersed-
ing the claim of Bahadur Shah's elder son, Mirza Fakhruddin, who
had been recognized by the British as heir-apparent. Bahadur Shah
endorsed the queen's aspirations, but the British, who had usurped
the right to nominate the heir-apparent, refused to consider their
wish. In 1856, Mirza Fakhruddin died. A new opportunity arose for
the Begum to press her son's claim, but the British chose the next
surviving son, Mohammad Koeash, as the successor. Zeenat Mahal
Begum was, however, not a woman to give in easily. Holding court
in her haveli with her favourite advisers, she conspired and in-
trigued to fulfil her plans. There is evidence that she could be ruthless in her pursuit. It was perhaps not a coincidence that all those
who stood in the way of her son's nomination died suddenly and
of mysterious causes, all within a year: Sir H. M. Eliott, British Agent
in Delhi (1823–6); James Thomason, the Lieutenant-Governor of the
North West Province; and Sir Thomas Metcalfe. To begin with Mirza
Fakhruddin's death was equally inexplicable. The British believed
that they had all been killed by 'vegetable poisons prepared in such
a way as to leave no trace behind them—a secret well known to the
famous Hakeems or native doctors'.[2]

During the revolt of 1857, the Begum was suspected of negotiating with the British. The deal was that she would facilitate their return, provided they agreed to recognize her son's claim to the throne. Angry troopers, who claimed to have proof of these parleys, attempted to storm her haveli. The solid wooden gates however held out. When the British recaptured the city in September 1857, Bahadur Shah Zafar and Begum Zeenat Mahal were incarcerated for almost a year in two separate rooms in the Red Fort, 'providing a peep show for any European who chose to stand and stare, from the wife of the Commissioner downwards'.[3] On 7 October 1858, the Begum bade a final farewell to her beloved Delhi and to Zeenat Mahal haveli, to accompany her husband, exiled by the British, to distant Rangoon. As the caravan set out on its long and arduous journey, and the ramparts of Shahjahanabad grew faint in the early morning haze, her thoughts must have echoed those of Zafar:

Kitna hai badnasib Zafar, dafn ke liye
Do gaz zamin bhi mil na saki ku-e-yaar mein

How unfortunate is Zafar, to not even possess
Two yards in the beloved's street, for his final rest.

All property belonging to the royal family was seized by the British. Zeenat Mahal haveli was bestowed upon Maharaja Narendar Singh, the ruler of Patiala, who had aided the British in quelling the revolt. For several decades after, the haveli remained in the possession

83

of the Patiala family. During the Second World War, the British administration occupied it as a tenant, converting it into a food ration office. Subsequently, it was taken over by a government school. Elderly residents recall the makeshift tents that were set up in the garden of the haveli to accommodate the spill over of students from the main building.

Thereafter, the haveli lingered on in graceful desuetude, witness to many more changes. In 1905, a tram line was laid in front of its gates. In the early 1950s, electric bulbs replaced the kerosene lamps on the street leading up to it. For the Patiala royal family, Begum Zeenat Mahal's *aashiana* (retreat) slowly became a liability. Years of neglect had taken their toll. The building was declared unsafe. The government acquired the premises, demolished the main part of the haveli and in 1974, built in its place, a government school for girls.

The school's address is still Zeenat Mahal. However, none of the children who study there today, seem to know who she was.

NOTES

1   Bahadur Shah, the last Mughal Emperor's poetic *nom de plume.*
2   Percival Spear, *Twilight of the Mughuls,* London, 1951, p. 163.
3   Ibid., p. 226.

The British Residency

منعم نے بنا ظلم کی رکھ گھر تو بنا یا

پر آپ کوئی رات ہی مہمان لہے گا

The ruler built his house
on the foundation of his might,
But he will dwell in it,
for but a few nights.

Meer Taqi Meer

IN SEPTEMBER 1803, a battle of considerable significance took place in
a village called Patparganj, across the river Jamuna from Delhi. British
forces under Lord Lake defeated the Marathas for the *de facto* control
of Delhi, while Shah Alam, the titular Mughal Emperor, watched
the progress of the battle from a balcony of the Red Fort. On
16 September 1803, Lord Lake was granted an audience by Shah
Alam. The infrastructure of British control was quickly established.
The Mughal king was made a British pensioner and his personal
allowance fixed at eleven and a half lakh rupees a year. On the out-
skirts of Kashmiri Gate, along the banks of the Jamuna, a British
Resident settled down to oversee British control. The house which
he occupied was the British Residency.

The mansion was not constructed anew. There was an existing
haveli of considerable renown and lineage which the British merely
converted to their use. This haveli belonged to Dara Shikoh
(1615) the eldest and favourite son of Shah Jahan. Dara Shikoh was
a learned man with an eclectic mind. He authored a book on com-
parative religion—*Majmua-ul-Baharain* and one on sufi practices. He
had the *Yoga Vasistha*, the *Bhagvad Gita*, and the Upanishads translated into Persian. He was also a poet. During his lifetime, his haveli
became a symbol of religious tolerance. In his search for spiritual
truth, he would invite men of learning to his home with whom
discussions on the unity of religions and on metaphysics would
continue late into the night. European missionaries were also among
the invitees. There is evidence that a Jesuit priest, Father Buzee, was
one of Dara's good friends.

Dara lost the battle to his younger brother, Aurangzeb, to succeed Shah Jahan to the throne. He was arrested, clothed in rags and paraded through the streets of Shahjahanabad, and then beheaded on 30 August 1659. Little is known of the fate of his haveli for the next century and a half, until the British took it over in 1803.

It is interesting to consider why the British made adaptations to an existing structure and did not build an edifice of their own. Firstly, Delhi for them was still virgin territory and the times were uncertain. It was perhaps too early to build new, permanent structures. Secondly, a battle had been won, and administrative control had to be established straightaway, under continuing military threat from enemies. Thirdly, and perhaps most importantly, they found the existing structure suitable to their needs; this was the phase when they were seeking to adapt to local circumstance, and were open to, if not appreciative of, indigenous models.

The compromise was to accept what existed, but give it a British stamp. This was achieved by adding the familiar classic columns to create a new facade for the haveli. Today, one can see the double row of stone pillars of the original haveli, standing some six yards behind the later collonaded facade. These pillars have been whitewashed and the space between the delicate arches cemented. Seen even more clearly from the rear of the building, under a magnificent banyan tree, are the forlorn, red stone pillars and arches of Dara's home, now partially concealed by cement walls. One portion of the original tehkhana is miraculously still open. If you have the courage to step into it, you can see clearly the delicately vaulted structure supported by graceful pillars.

Ochterlony enjoying a nautch in his haveli.

The first British Resident in Delhi was the flamboyant David

The Residency, with its typical colonnaded facade, as it stands today. The building now houses the Archaeology Department of the Delhi Administration.

Ochterlony who had commanded a regiment under Lord Lake and was later his Deputy Adjutant General. He ensconced himself in the Residency in the style of a Mughal nawab. A painting at the Residency shows him in rich Indian attire, seated in the traditional manner on the floor, smoking a hookah and enjoying a nautch. He had a harem of thirteen Indian wives who would often go out together on elephant back to take the air. His income was rumoured to be in the vicinity of fifteen thousand rupees a month, a princely sum for those days, but his extravagant lifestyle ensured that all of it was spent. Bishop Heber once met Ochterlony's cortege on the way to Bharatpur and had occasion to witness the paraphernalia of pomp with which he surrounded himself:

There certainly was a very considerable number of led horses, elephants, palanqueens and covered carriages. . . . There was an escort of two companies of infantry, a troop of regular cavalry, and I should guess forty or fifty irregulars, on horse and foot, armed with spears and matchlocks of all possible forms; the string of camels was a very long one, and the whole procession was what might pass in Europe for that of an eastern prince travelling. Sir David himself . . . was so wrapped up in shawls, kincob, fur, and a Mughal furred cap, that his face was all that was visible.[1]

The authority of the British Resident often rested more on clever psychological projection than on substantive strength. In terms of real military strength, Ochterlony had only one battalion and four companies of sepoys under him in Delhi. The power base of the *gora sahebs* was, as 1857 would dramatically show later, always fragile. However, this inherent weakness was camouflaged by the ambience of authority and grandeur. The British Resident was at the fulcrum of this power play; the Residency was his stage. Extant picture of the mansion show that it was maintained lavishly. Manicured lawns, as part of an extensive garden estate, surrounded it. It is probable that another abandoned haveli, once of importance, was located inside the Residency estate. This belonged to Shah Jahan's contemporary, Ali Mardan Khan, who had built the Nahar-i-Bihisht, the famous canal flowing through the city and the Red Fort.

David Ochterlony was twice Resident at Delhi, from 1803 to 1806, and again from 1819 to 1822. He was the only Englishman whose Mughal title, Nasir-ud-daulah, gave its name to a cantonment town—Nasirabad in Rajasthan. He died in Delhi in 1825, after having spent almost five decades in India.

Another Englishman who lived in the Residency was the legendary Charles Metcalfe. He became Resident in 1811 at the age of twenty-seven, and for the next eight years was the *de facto* king of Delhi. He was less flamboyant and more Victorian in deportment. To the English and Europeans in Delhi he was a father figure, and during his tenure, the Residency acquired for them the image of a benevolent anchorage. Like Ochterlony, he had many of the attributes of the Mughal umrah. He spoke and read excellent Persian, smoked the hookah, and had his Indian *bibis* (wives), whom he kept in another house in the nearby Shalimar Garden. The house was known as 'Metcalfe Saheb ki Kothi' and he had at least three Eurasian sons. In administrative matters he was punctilious. It is said that to avoid importunity he would leave the Residency as little as possible, preferring to take his daily walk on its roof.

A rear view of the Residency. Notice the red sandstone and marble work, and the arches—remanents of the earlier haveli modified by the British for their use.

Bookshelves scattered aimlessly, witness like the columns, to another era, stand a forlorn vigil.

OPPOSITE:

The small marble plaque says it all.

In later life, Metcalfe became the Lieutenant-Governor of the North West Provinces (1836–8), Governor of Jamaica (1839–42), and Governor-General of Canada (1843–5). But memories of his stay in Delhi, distilled from many an evening spent quietly at the Residency, watching the Red Fort looming majestically in the distance and the flickering lights of the city beyond, would haunt him. 'The ruins of grandeur', he wrote, 'that extend for miles on every side fill the mind with serious reflection. The palaces crumbling into dust, the vast mausoleums . . . these things cannot be looked at with indifference.'[2]

The Residency became the pioneering focus of an expanded British settlement around and beyond the Kashmiri Gate. The years from 1803 to 1857 were the years of 'frozen peace', a period of enforced

political stability, an extended lull before the storm of 1857. Taking advantage of the relative security, people began to build outside the city walls, between the Kashmiri Gate and the Ridge. Next to the Residency, the construction of St. James's Church began in 1826. Col James Skinner built his house opposite the church. The Dak Bungalow, the Kacheri, the offices of the Treasury, the Post Office and the Customs House came up nearby. Major landmarks were Ludlow Castle, the house of the noted surgeon, Dr Ludlow, and on the Ridge, the haveli of the Maratha nobleman, Hindu Rao. Further away was Metcalfe House, built by Sir Thomas Metcalfe. There were also several officers' bungalows, including that of Sir John Lawrence when he was posted in Delhi from 1831 to 1838.

In 1832, the Residency ceased to be the home of the British Resident in Delhi. In that year the Resident was redesignated as Civil Commissioner and Agent to the Governor-General at Delhi. William Fraser, the first Commissioner and Agent, preferred to live in Hindu Rao's mansion on the Ridge. The Residency became the seat of the Delhi College, and from then onwards was used almost continuously for educational purposes.

Today, the Delhi College of Engineering is located in the Residency's erstwhile gardens. The mansion itself still stands, but in considerable disrepair. It is now the office of the Delhi unit of the Archaeological Survey of India. A small marble tablet on the western face of the building says simply: ONCE THE RESIDENCY.

NOTES

1   Quoted in M. A. Laird (ed.), *Bishop Heber in Northern India*, Cambridge, 1971, pp. 260–1.
2   Quoted in Philip Woodruffe, *The Men who Ruled India*, vol. I, London, 1953, p. 272.

Skinner's House

وہی جنگل وہی صیّاد وہی بجلی کا خوف

دنیا ہی بدل دی ہے تعمیرِ نشیمن نے

'Tis the same jungle,
    the same hunter at hunt
    the same fear of lightning
But, the building of my nest
Has changed all in my reckoning.

JAMES SKINNER, BORN in 1778, was the son of Lt-Col Hercules Skinner, a Scotsman, and a Rajput lady. At the age of sixteen, after working three days at a printer's firm in Calcutta, he ran away to become a soldier. When he was eighteen, he joined the Maratha army under the French mercenary Count de Boigne, and remained with it till the age of twenty-five. That was the year when the British fought the Marathas for the occupation of Delhi, the seat of the Mughal empire. Skinner then switched his allegiance to the British. Being half Indian, he could not, under a new British decree, be given a regular officer's Commission. However, he was allowed to raise a contingent of 'Irregular Horse'. This body of cavalry, known as 'Skinners Horse', accompanied the victorious British troops under Lord Lake into Delhi in 1803.

In the decades that followed, 'Skinners Horse' emerged as a crack unit, trouble-shooting for the British across north India. A contemporary recorded that 'they are reckoned, by all the English in this' part of the country, the most useful and trusty, as well as the boldest body of men in India'.[1] Indeed, the reputation and prestige of James Skinner grew immeasurably. The British granted him a jagir yielding twenty thousand rupees a year, appointed him Lt-Col in His Majesty's service, and gave him an honorary title. The Mughal king had separately bestowed upon him the title: 'Nasir-ud-daulah Ghalib Jang' (Most Exalted, Victorious in War). The time had come for Skinner to take his place among the umara of Delhi, and to build for himself a mansion that befitted his wealth and status.

For its location he chose Kashmiri Gate, which was then fast

One of the few remaining pictures of Skinner's house.

Skinner presiding over his durbar.

developing into the most fashionable hub for the European elite. His house came up a stone's throw away from the British Residency. The Telegraph Office, the Civil Courts, the Treasury, the beautiful bungalow of Thomas Metcalfe and other residences of British officials such as the Judge, and the Civil Surgeon were all nearby. A furlong away was the building which housed the office of the only local British newspaper—the *Delhi Gazette*. Also published from there was the *Delhi Sketchbook* a gossip sheet on both Delhi as well as 'back home'.

Opposite his haveli, Skinner built the magnificent St. James's Church. According to lore, he had taken a vow, as he lay wounded on the battlefield, that he would build a church were he to be rescued. The very next morning, so the story goes, a woman, quite unexpectedly, brought succour in the form of food and water. However, Skinner does not refer, in his memoirs, to his taking such a vow. Another version is that Skinner discovered a ruined mosque in the compound of his house and had it restored (it still stands today). Following this the Hindu members of his zenana persuaded him to build a small temple, which he did. Having built the mosque and temple, he now felt it necessary, in loyalty to his own faith, to build a church.

The church took a long time to complete. Bishop Heber, who visited Delhi in 1824, noted that it was being constructed. Perhaps one reason for the slow progress was that Skinner was, in spite of his vast land holdings, short of cash. He was a bad investor and had lost a great deal of money in 1831, in the slump of the indigo market and the collapse of Alexander's Bank in Calcutta. Moreover, he had

95

miscalculated his costs which were more than twice the initial estimate of Rs 90,000. However, in 1836, Bishop Daniel Wilson, who was in Delhi *en route* to Simla, consecrated the church, after which the entire European and Anglo-Indian community gathered at Skinner's residence to express their deep gratitude.

Although Skinner aspired for acceptance within the European community, he lived very much like a Mughal nawab. But in this he was not very different from his European contemporaries in India who unconsciously fell into what Percival Spear has called the cult of the Mughal dignitary or omrah. Skinner's mansion emulated the British modification of the original haveli structure. It had a classical facade, with high collonades, akin to Begum Samru's palace and the first British Residency. Behind the classical frontage, was the same organic structure of an upfront mardanah, and the zenana at the back, complete with Bengali style apartments for the ladies and marble bathrooms in the Mughal pattern. The house was surrounded by a beautiful garden laid out by Skinner himself. There were several fountains, and at least one circular pavilion in the midst of a large circular water tank.

The flamboyance in Skinner's personality was linked to his Rajput lineage, and to a larger-than-life image created by stories of his valour on the battlefield. Men of his Company—Skinner's Horse—were a familiar sight in Delhi, and were described by Bishop Heber as 'the most showy and picturesque cavaliers, I have seen since I was in the south of Russia. They had turbans of dark red shawl, long yellow caftans (which gave them the label of the "yellow boys"),

96

ABOVE:

The mosque, once within the precincts of Skinner's mansion, facing the church which was situated outside.

BELOW:

Col James Skinner in formal military attire.

with dark red cummerbunds, and trousers of the same colour.'[2] His circle of friends was large, including the most well known personalities of Delhi such as Ochterlony, the first British Resident, Charles Metcalfe who succeeded him, Charles' younger brother Thomas Metcalfe, later Commissioner and Agent, Begum Samru and members of the Indian nobility. William Fraser, the British Resident who was murdered in 1835, was a particularly close friend, and lies buried in the compound of St. James's Church. Skinner had erected over Fraser's grave, at a cost of Rs 10,000, a beautiful tomb of white marble inlaid with green stones, representing the weeping willow.

Skinner's hospitality was legendary. A visit to his haveli was a must on the agenda of any distinguished visitor to Delhi. A contemporary, James Baillie Fraser, wrote:

It was his [Skinner's] joy to assemble a knot of friends at his home at Delhi and many a pleasant day, and week, and month was spent with 'Old Secunder' in the pastimes or pursuits which then made India so delightful and which he so well knew how to promote. The joyous excursions that were made amongst the interesting environs of Dehlee, when pitching our tents amidst ruins that extend for twenty miles around it—now at the mausoleum of Hoomayoon, now at the gigantic pillar of the Coatab, or again among the Cyclopean walls and speaking silence of the old city of Toghlucabad, till the evening saw us all gaily seated round our well spread table, hookahs in mouth, enjoying the comforts of excellent fare, and no less pleasant converse—these were enjoyments which none who partook of them will ever forget.[3]

Skinner's haveli was famous for the nautch performances he would arrange for his guests. One European visitor to Delhi, invited to

97

Skinner's in the evening, assumed without doubt that 'Mr Skinner would, of course, have the best [dancing girls] that could be procured.'[4] Lord Auckland's sisters—Emily and Fanny Eden—were also present at a wonderful nautch at his place. An elegant marble stage had been set up on the side of the house, where both Hindu and Muslim women sang ghazals in Persian and performed stories from the Hindu texts. For those on whom a nautch girl left a particularly deep impression, the good Colonel would arrange to have a small painting of her ready for them at the time of departure.

It should not be assumed that enjoying nautches and entertaining his friends was all that Skinner did when not on the field. He was the author of a classic work on Indian castes, tribes and religion— *Tashrih-ul-Akram* (A Concise Account of the People). Another of his works—*Tazkirat-ul-Umara* (A Description of the Princes)—was a comprehensive compilation of, and commentary on, the principal chiefs of Hindustan. But in spite of his many accomplishments, and notwithstanding his obvious utility to the British, for them Skinner would remain a social aspirant, a lovable curiosity but never an equal.

The following comment by Emily Bayley is corroborative:

Colonel Skinner was a man of dark blood, and his wife was a native lady, and their children were all, of course very dark in complexion, and spoke English with an extraordinary accent, and the whole family was a marvellous revelation to anyone fresh from England . . . although they looked upon themselves as English people and held a prominent position in Delhi society they had very little education and were more native than English in their ways.[5]

98

OPPOSITE AND ABOVE:

Some remnants of Skinner's mansion, probably the outhouses, which have escaped demolition. It is said that the circular building above was once a baradari standing in the midst of a pool.

James Skinner died on 4 December 1841, at his family estate in Hansi. Some months later his coffin was disinterred and brought, escorted by his Regiment, to Delhi. 'Here the cortege was met by a multitude from the city, so vast, the natives said, that no emperor of Hindustan, was ever brought into Delhi in such state as Sikander Sahib.'[6] As the coffin was laid to rest at St. James's Church, sixty-three guns were fired on the British Resident's orders, one for each year of his life.

Skinner's family continued to live in Skinner's house till the Revolt of 1857, when it was taken over by the rebellious troopers. The fifth or Reserve Column under Brigadier Longfield drove the 'mutineers' out of the house on 14 September 1857. Initially used as barracks for troops, the haveli soon after became the Mess House of the Queen's Regiment. Later it housed the Bank of Bengal, and still later was acquired by the East India Railways. In the 1890s the house was bought by the rich banker Lala Sultan Singh, who in turn, sold it to Hindu College. Skinner's bathroom was used by the college as its staff-room. When Hindu College was allotted land on the Delhi University campus, it surrendered the building to the Delhi municipal administration. For a while the house was used as a Kacheri. Today, almost no trace is left of it, as the main building has been demolished to build a multi-storeyed structure for the water and sewage offices of the Municipal Corporation of Delhi.

St. James's Church, however, continues to survive. It was almost destroyed in 1857, but was subsequently restored. In its compound, within a wrought iron enclosure, are the graves of the descendants

101

of James Skinner. In spite of being maintained by the Mission authorities, depredation has taken place here as well. The tombstone of Sir Thomas Metcalfe, in the church garden, was also destroyed by vandals in 1974. The bullet ridden original orb and cross of the church, remnant of the attack on the church in 1857, were stolen in 1955.

The interior of the church—a living tribute to the man who made it.

NOTES

1   Quoted in M.A. Laird (ed.), *Bishop Heber in Northern India*, Cambridge, 1971, p. 224.
2   Ibid., p. 224.
3   James Baillie Fraser, *Military Memoir of Colonel James Skinner*, London, 1851.
4   R. B. Minturn, *From New York to Delhi*, London, 1858.
5   Emily Bayley, *Memoirs*, quoted in M. M. Kaye, *The Golden Calm*, New York, 1980, p. 166.
6   Dennis Holman, *Sikander Sahib*, London, 1961.

Metcalfe Saheb ki Haveli

جن کی تعمیرِ عشق کرتا ہے
کون رہتا ہے ان مکانوں میں

Who lives in those mansions
which love has constructed?

Firaq

The frontage of Metcalfe House—as it originally was.

O<small>UTSIDE</small> <small>KASHMIRI</small> <small>GATE</small>, very near the river Jamuna, stands a handsome building which now houses the Defence Science Research Laboratory. Entry to it is, for reasons of security, extremely restricted. But you can get an adequate glimpse of it from Ring Road, as you drive towards Model Town from the Inter State Bus Terminus.

This building was once the beloved haveli of Thomas Metcalfe, British Agent and Commissioner in Delhi from 1835 to 1853. Although greatly damaged and ransacked in 1857, the building was renovated later and even today, the extant structure bears a similarity in broad outline and spatial features to the original mansion designed and constructed by Metcalfe Saheb.

Thomas Theophilius Metcalfe arrived in Delhi in 1813, following the footsteps of his illustrious elder brother Sir Charles Metcalfe, who twice served as British Resident in Delhi. The younger Metcalfe made Delhi his home, living there for forty years until his death in 1853. The haveli that he built for himself in the 1830s was regarded as one of the sights in northern India and, as per British records, was the most expensive house in its time in the North West Province.

Thomas Metcalfe acquired his estate, stretching over 187 acres, from the villagers of Chandrawal who were in possession of a strategic strip of territory from the Ridge to the Jamuna. He was not very good with his finances; many of his debts had to be settled by his elder and more responsible brother Charles, who dubbed him 'exceedingly improvident'. When Thomas began to build his mansion, Charles referred to it as the 'Folly of the House', and was afraid that the means used to finance it might not be entirely honourable. There was this whiff of suspicion that Thomas had borrowed from a private banker in violation of government rules. However, rumour did not become scandal, and in 1835, soon after the house had been completed, Thomas Metcalfe succeeded the murdered William Fraser as the Agent and Commissioner of Delhi.

His mansion was built in the typical pre-1857 classical style. Handsome stone columns—so typical of the facade in a classical structure—supported a wide verandah, 20 to 30 ft wide, which ran all around the building. The frontage was distinguished by a bay-room which obviously received a great deal of the sun in winter since it was used in that season as a breakfast room. The river Jamuna, which has now moved away from the house, once flanked the gardens on the eastern side of the mansion. The more formal rooms—study, library, dining-room, drawing-room—were clustered together on the north-east side.

The more private rooms—a family dining-room and drawing-room, bedrooms, baths and dressing-rooms—were on the north-west side. This categorical separation of the public and private areas was not the only feature borrowed from the traditional haveli structure. In fact, early British buildings were often additions to or alterations of existing havelis, the most notable example of this being the adaption of Dara Shikoh and Ali Mardan Khan's haveli to house the first British Residency.

Moreover, the climate to which the British were particularly sensitive, provided a uniform conditioning imperative in the construction of both the 'native' haveli and its bungalow off-shoot. The need to

Metcalfe House today.

guard against the searing summer heat necessitated thick walls and high ceilings. The ceilings in Metcalfe's house were 24 ft high. The presence of a large central chamber—seen clearly in Metcalfe's house—has led Percival Spear to argue that the basic plan was 'possibly borrowed in part from that of the Muslim tomb, consisting of a large central chamber with lower surrounding rooms and verandahs'.[1] The tehkhana or underground apartment was another feature taken from the haveli. Metcalfe's mansion had two: a 'principal' tehkhana which he used during the hottest months, and a second tehkhana used as a billiard room. It is my belief that the verandah—such an ubiquitous part of British colonial construction—was in basic inspiration an attempt to transplant in a bungalow format the semi-enclosed feature of the daalan and dardaalan in the haveli. This view is reinforced by the fact that the part of the verandah which flanked the private areas of the house, remained an extension of the private area, though on the periphery. The verandah, as a kind of modified daalan, fulfilled the desire to have in a house, space that was private and yet not enclosed. Thomas Metcalfe's house also had a *chabootra*—a flat platform outside the house, which was a variation of the more formal garden pavilion or baradari.

Metcalfe spent a fortune furnishing his haveli. His furniture was of mahogany and rosewood, and many of his tables were of marble. His library consisted of 25,000 books, each bound impeccably in Russian leather. He had a special fondness for engravings and his daughter recalls that each room was adorned with portraits as well as portrayals of historical events. He also had an excellent collection of clocks, silver inkstands and paper knives.

BELOW AND OPPOSITE TOP:
A view of the haveli from the eastern side, overlooking the river Jamuna, as it was then and as it is today.

Among the formal rooms was Metcalfe's famous Napoleon Gallery. Emily Bayley, his daughter, has recorded for posterity a description of this remarkable room:

The room called the Napoleon Gallery, which was in the north-east corner of the house, was entirely devoted to the memory of Napoleon Bonaparte, of whom, as I have said, my Father was a devoted admirer. Its bookcases were filled with all the best and most interesting works relating to his life and career, and the walls were covered with fine engravings: portraits of the great hero, of his generals, and of all the events of his life. In one corner of the room on a marble pedestal stood Canova's marble bust of Napoleon, a beautiful work of art of which I now possess only the broken pieces, which I gathered out of the ruins of the house at Delhi two years after the Mutiny.

The centre and side tables in the Napoleon Gallery were covered with beautiful bronzes and statuettes, all connected with the history of the emperor. One especially fine bronze, three feet long, depicted the fight of the Bridge of Lodi, but this, like everything else, was either destroyed or carried off on the day the house was looted in the middle of May 1857. On the centre table, under a glass case, there was a beautiful marble stand with an exquisite silver statuette of Napoleon, . . .[2]

It was obvious that Metcalfe thoroughly enjoyed his haveli. He utilized every part of it for the various aspects of his lifestyle. His day began at five in the morning when he would have his *chota haziri* (early breakfast) in the verandah. As he strolled about in the verandah, servants would come to him to receive the instructions for the day. When annoyed with a servant, he would send for a pair of white kid gloves which were brought to him on a silver salver. With grave ceremony, he would put on the gloves and gently pinch the ear of the unfortunate offender. At seven he went for his bath for which he had built, in addition to the bathrooms in the house, a swimming bath just outside the verandah. This too was an attempt to emulate the elaborate marble baths found in the palace and in many havelis of the umara in the city. Prayers in the Oratory and breakfast at eight o'clock sharp would be followed by a half-hour satisfying smoke in the main dining-room. His hookah of solid silver had an embossed cup with silver chains hanging from it and a beautifully carved mouthpiece. The smoke over, he would repair to his study to write letters, and then leave for office punctually at ten. The afternoons were spent reading in the Napoleon Gallery. For a break he had a game of billiards in the tehkhana, after which he would settle himself for several hours on the chabootra overhanging the river, receiving friends or amusing himself with flying his large collection of pigeons, until dinner was announced. Dinner was served in the best of China—Derby, Worcester, Chinese porcelain—and everything, 'even the trays and saucepans' were of solid silver. Once a month he gave a dinner party for about twelve to sixteen people, on which occasions the gardens of Metcalfe House would be splendidly lit up with coloured lamps.

In 1844, Sir Thomas created his country house near the Qutb. A country retreat was popular with British officials; both Ochterlony, the first British Resident, and Charles Metcalfe who succeeded him, had one, the latter's at Shalimar Bagh, known as 'Metcalfe Saheb ki Kothi'. Thomas Metcalfe's country house was unique. The original

Metcalfe House, burnt and looted during the Revolt of 1857 (ABOVE); Thomas Metcalfe's resplendent tehkhanas when the house was in its glory (LEFT AND FACING PAGE RIGHT).

structure was a tomb, octagonal in shape, with a large central dome and surrounded by a wide verandah. Metcalfe, who had bought the tomb, left the lower part of the structure as it was, but converted the verandah to house a library, a drawing-room, three bedrooms, a dressing-room, an oratory, and two entrance halls, at the eastern and western ends, which could be reached by separate flights of stairs from outside. He named his retreat 'Dilkusha' (the Delight of the Heart), and landscaped a beautiful garden around it with three or four rooms 'for the accommodation of gentlemen'. His daughter writes:

...as my Father's favourite amusement was brick and mortar, he designed and built at some distance off, on high ground, a light-house and a small fort—or, rather, a building that looked like a fort, with a castellated wall. These created a diversion from the level monotony of the rocky ground and, as my Father always had a light put in each of the buildings on the nights that we stayed at the Dilkusha, we could see the buildings as we sat on the chabootra of an evening....[3]

Thomas Metcalfe died in 1853, possibly of poisoning. He had refused to recognize the claim of Jiwan Bakht—the son of Zeenat Mahal, Bahadur Shah Zafar's youngest and favourite wife—to be heir-apparent. There was a suspicion that Zeenat Mahal was involved in his mysterious death. Theophilius Metcalfe, his son, who was Chief Magistrate of Delhi, stayed on in the house until 1857, when the Revolt broke. The Gujars of Chandrawal, from whom Metcalfe had, by all accounts, arbitrarily bought his estate, seized the opportunity to avenge themselves. The house was set on fire; its

prized possessions looted and mercilessly vandalized. Metcalfe's son managed to make a dramatic escape with the help of friends, his face blackened to disguise him as an Indian *sawar* (trooper). Only a charred skeletal framework remained of Metcalfe's beloved haveli.

The mansion lived on as a famous ruin, until in 1913, it was reconstructed in the Gothic style which came into vogue after 1857. No trace remained of its original classical facade. Since it was located strategically, it was taken over by the army. Most of the land surrounding it was acquired by the government for the temporary capital in 1912. During the Second World War, the haveli was turned into an army officer's residence. Ironically, the great-great-grandson of Thomas Metcalfe, Lt-Col John Ricketts, was allotted quarters in it. Following independence, Metcalfe House became, until 1959, the Academy for the training of civil service recruits.

It was an emotional experience for Lt-Col Ricketts to live in the house built by his famous ancestor. He wrote,

Houses often have a kind of aura, sensed when inside them. There is an atmosphere attributable to the personality of someone who has built his house on a chosen spot and dwelt in it with his family for a spell of time. . . . The pattern of all had changed, except for two great underground rooms (Metcalfe's tehkhanas) which were filled with lumber. . . . The house seemed to have accepted its fate, as though that were no fault of its owner. There were no ghosts, and it was pervaded by a sort of calm.[4]

NOTES

1   Percival Spear, *Twilight of the Mughuls*, London, 1951, p. 150.
2   Emily Bayley, *Memoirs*, quoted in M. M. Kaye, *The Golden Calm*, New York, 1980, p. 127.
3   Ibid., p. 148.
4   Lt-Col John Mildmay Ricketts' 'Introduction' in M. M. Kaye, *The Golden Calm*, New York, 1980, p. 12.

Haveli Ahsanullah Khan

دیدنی ہے شکستگی دل کی

کیا عمارت غموں نے ڈھائی ہے

It is worth watching
How my heart was vanquished
What a mansion indeed
Grief has demolished.

Meer Taqi Meer

The outer entrance to the haveli, off Hauz Qazi boulevard (ABOVE LEFT); Inayat Pavilion, later converted into the Excelsior Cinema(ABOVE RIGHT); the inner wall of the haveli complex (OPPOSITE).

Hakim Ahsanullah Khan was the personal physician to the last Mughal Emperor, Bahadur Shah Zafar. His importance in the royal court was, however, much more than that of a royal physician. He was the king's closest adviser, his trusted confidant, and a good friend. Given this, it is not surprising that his haveli occupied pride of place in the walled city.

Indeed, the haveli was more of a palace, covering an entire mohalla over several thousand square yards. Its main entrance was located off Hauz Qazi, next to the present Excelsior Cinema. The area where the theatre stands was the mardanah. Towards the back of the theatre was a more private area, once an exquisite complex of Turkish baths, gardens, and guest-houses where men of importance, including the king's guests, often stayed. Behind this was the zenana. This was a particularly beautiful structure with carved doorways and stained-glass ornamentation on the arch above. Several interconnected rooms were separated by thick silk curtains. Expensive Persian carpets covered the floor, while the ceiling, remnants of which could be seen till a few months ago, was intricately carved in wood. It is said that the artist who did the roof of the Diwan-i-Khas, in the Red Fort, was responsible for the ceiling of this haveli too. *Khutbas*—snatches of panegyrics—engraved in marble, adorned the mansion's outer walls. A branch of the main canal, the Nahar-i-Bihisht, flowed through the haveli complex. It is also believed that a secret underground tunnel led from the haveli to the Red Fort.

The Great Revolt of 1857 against the British broke out in Delhi in May, when the Sawars from Meerut came riding into the city and forced the aged and ailing Mughal king to assume the leadership of the revolt. Most British officers and their wives and children were ruthlessly murdered. For the next four months the troopers were masters of Shahjahanabad. Anyone suspected of collaborating with the British was summarily dealt with. Hakim Ahsanullah Khan was suspected of having clandestine negotiations with the British. Many other members of the court were also under suspicion, since it was no secret that the king had endorsed the rebellion reluctantly. Anger against alleged 'informers' became specially virulent when the rebel forces suffered defeat in battle at the hands of the British. On

7 August 1857, an ammunition store in the city blew up. Troops led by one of the Mughal princes stormed into the Diwan-i-Khas of the Red Fort seeking to arrest the Hakim on the grounds that he was a British agent. Initially, the king refused to hand him over. However, he later agreed on the condition that the Hakim would not be harmed but merely confined to house-arrest. Even so, the king could not prevent the angry mob from plundering the Hakim's haveli. A contemporary has recorded:

They looted his palace, adorned in beauty like a Chinese painting, and set fire to the roof. Every beam and every joist, joined in that roof as firmly as the stone set in the ring, fell and was burnt to ashes. The walls were blackened with smoke, as though the palace itself had put on black to mourn its own destruction.[1]

Hakim Ahsanullah Khan was among a handful of Muslim noblemen who survived when the British recaptured the city and unleashed an orgy of ruthless reprisals. Mirza Ghalib, the great poet, has chronicled in his letters, the plight of the impoverished nobility. Ghalib and Ahsanullah Khan were close friends. In fact, the stipend that Ghalib received to write a historical account of the Mughal dynasty was largely due to Ahsanullah Khan's influence with the king. Ghalib's house in Gali Ballimaran was close by to the Hakim's haveli. Both shared a love of poetry. In a letter written in 1856, Ghalib lamented that apart from the Hakim he was surrounded by people who knew nothing of poetry.

Though the Hakim's property was only temporarily seized by the British and returned, the old style of living could never be restored. Ghalib has recorded this pithy account:

BELOW:

The long chhatta leading from the outside to the more private areas of the haveli.

OPPOSITE:

The great poet Mirza Ghalib, who was a close friend of Hakim Ahsanullah Khan, lived close by. The picture shows the pitiable condition of the daalan, where it is said, Ghalib loved to sit while composing his verses.

Hakim Ahsanullah Khan has obtained possession of his houses. There is an Englishman living in the zenana, at the back of the baths. He pays a rent of thirty-five rupees a month. . . . Ahsanullah Khan has moved into his house. He has turned the main hall into the zenana, and made his own quarters where the stable used to be.[2]

After Hakim Ahsanullah Khan's death, which was probably in the early 1870s, his haveli, or what remained of it, was bought from his descendants by one Ikramullah Khan, who, by 'native' stand-ards, was an important functionary in the city administration. In fact, local inhabitants prefaced Ikramullah Khan's name by the honorific title 'Deputy' (a title used even today in the lower levels of moffusil administration in India), and the immediate area around the haveli began to be known as 'Deputy Ikramullah Khan Mohalla'. In the 1890s Ikramullah Khan's daughter married Nawab Abul Hasan Khan, the grandson of Mufti Sadruddin Azurda, one of the well known personalities of Delhi during the final years of Mughal rule, and a great friend and contemporary of Hakim Ahsanullah Khan and Ghalib.

'Azurda' was the Mufti's *takhallus* or pen-name, for he was a good poet. He was also, as the title 'Mufti' indicates, the judge in the local judiciary. The story goes that on one occasion, Ghalib was produced in his court for defaulting on payment of debts. The Mufti asked Ghalib if he had anything to say in his defence. Ghalib merely narrated the couplet:

Indeed I drank on credit but also knew for sure
My spend-thrift poverty one day my ruin would procure.[3]

Nawab Sikandar Hasan Khan, the present occupant of the haveli.

A window long barricaded from its past.

The Mufti smiled, passed the order against Ghalib, and paid the money due, from his own pocket. Azurda's adopted son, Inayat-ur-Rehman, joined the Nizam's court in Hyderabad. There is a story, whose veracity I have not been able to establish, that the famous 'Nizam' diamond was a gift from Inayat-ur-Rehman. It is, however, a fact, that till recently Inayat-ur-Rehman's descendants received a monthly stipend from the Nizam's estates, bequeathed by the latter in perpetuity, in appreciation for the gift of a diamond. Today, one can see, above the ugly tangle of electrical wires and cables, the words INAYAT PAVILION atop the entrance of the Excelsior Cinema.

Thus, when Abul Hasan married Deputy Ikramullah Khan's daughter, and moved in with his father-in-law, the ageing haveli, a trifle battered, but still graceful, became the stage on which some of Delhi's most distinguished lineages and personalities intermeshed. Abul Hasan Khan's son, Ghalib Hasan Khan (1920–86), was the next occupant. He was a colourful personality, very fond of imported cars in which he used to deal. His family claims that in 1957, he bought Sheikh Abdullah's 1932 model, white, bullet-proof Cadillac, in an auction in Bombay. Two remnants of his automobile collection remain in the haveli. A Sunbeam Talbot of 1946 is parked, sans wheels, inside the main courtyard. It stands atop the only visible portion of the canal that once flowed through the haveli complex. A Singer is buried somewhere in the debris of two rooms, unopened for decades.

Today, Hakim Ahsanullah Khan's haveli stands in irremediable desolation. Since a branch of the family had migrated to Pakistan after partition, the haveli remained for many years in the hands of the Custodian of Evacuee Property. The family retrieved it in 1963. Now a cluster of shops and workshops surrounds it on every side. The Turkish hammams lie buried under mounds of debris; intricate carvings have been plastered over; the beautiful zenana complex is being demolished even as I write this.

Nawab Sikandar Hasan Khan, son of Ghalib Hasan, is the present occupant. There is a doorbell now at the entrance of the haveli. Several minutes pass before someone hesitatingly opens the door. When you are ushered in, the Nawab Saheb, gracious and affable, offers you tea. You try not to notice that the cup is chipped.

NOTES

1 Ralph Russel and Khurshidul Islam, *Ghalib, 1797–1869*, vol. I: *Life and Letters*, London, 1969, p. 139.
2 Ibid., p. 213.
3 *Diwan-i-Ghalib*, trans. M. Mujeeb, *Mirza Ghalib*, New Delhi, 1970, p. 28.

The Haksar Haveli

مدتیں گذریں تری یاد بھی آئی نہ ہمیں

اور ہم بھول گئے ہوں تجھے ایسا بھی نہیں

Ages passed
And I did not remember you,
But it would be wrong to say also
That I had forgotten you.

Firaq

Extending north-westwards from Turkman Gate to Fatehpuri Masjid is an avenue called Sita Ram Bazaar. At a certain point it is met by Sarak Prem Narain. At this intersection stands the ruin of a haveli where on 8 February 1916, India's first Prime Minister, Jawaharlal Nehru, was married to Kamala.

Kamala's parents lived a short distance away from this haveli and had asked for the use of the haveli from one of the most distinguished Kashmiri families in Delhi—the Haksars—for the wedding. The first of the Haksars, the brothers Sahib Ram and Sita Ram (after whom the avenue is named), came to Delhi from Kashmir in 1804.[1] Their descendants acquired a reputation for scholarship and learning. Sahib Ram's grandson—Ram Kishen—studied at Delhi College, and was renowned for his knowledge of Sanskrit, Persian and Arabic. Sita Ram's great-grandsons—Sarup Narain, Dharm Narain and Prem Narain—were also luminaries of Delhi College, and rose to positions of considerable eminence. Sarup Narain became the Dewan of the royal state of Bundelkhand; Dharm Narain edited the Urdu weekly *Qiran-us-Sadyn* in Delhi and later the *Malwa Akhbar*,

Mr. & Mrs. Motilal Nehru request the pleasure of your company on the occasion of the marriage of their son Jawaharlal Nehru with Kamala Kaul, daughter of Pandit Jawaharmal Kaul, at Delhi, on the 7th February, 1916, and afterwards on February 8th and 9th, 1916.

Anand Bhavan.   An answer will oblige.

ABOVE:

The invitation card for the wedding.

LEFT:

Jawaharlal and Kamla on the day of their wedding.

an important publication in Indore; and Prem Narain, after whom the sarak is named, was appointed the Dewan of the wealthy state of Tehri.

The haveli was an imposing three-storeyed structure, with large halls and courtyards and a huge tehkhana. Apart from its social eminence, it was particularly suitable for the wedding because its many spacious rooms could accommodate the huge *baarat* (wedding party) that Motilal Nehru brought to Delhi for the marriage of his only son. Indeed, the guests turned out to be so many (a special Nehru wedding train had steamed into Delhi from Allahabad) that a Nehru wedding camp was set up near the Maidens Hotel to accommodate the spillover.

There is some evidence that the haveli had suffered damage in the Revolt of 1857 and been renovated in 1887. As befitting the rise in the fortunes of the family over the decades, the refurbished haveli had more grandiose features and richer construction material. It, therefore, appeared relatively new at the time of the wedding; its intrinsic beauty accentuated by the elaborate flower decoration and

illuminations that are the norm during weddings. A couplet in Persian on the beautifully ornamented gateway reads as follows: The interior of the haveli.

Chun bafazle aizdi taamir gashta-i-makan
Zahiri va maanvi zi misra haasil mi shavad
Nek zeba o khajasta fal hajri sale aan
Az masih haftad charo yak hazaro hasht zad

By the grace of God this house has been constructed.
And its apparent and inner beauty is brought out in this couplet.
Good and beautiful and auspicious is the moment in the hijri year.
A thousand eight hundred and eighty-seven in the Christian calendar.

Jawaharlal Nehru was not a great believer in rituals, but went through the long marriage ceremony with dignity and patience. After the wedding, the bride and bridegroom sat together for the ceremony of the worship of the flowers—*posh puja*. Nehru's sister, Vijaylakshmi Pandit, and other girls of the family, sang songs invoking the blessings of God. Sanskrit songs were fluently and effortlessly translated by Mrs Pandit into English, to the great appreciation of an audience, in which several British officials were present. The haveli was also the venue of a lavish dinner, an event not without its problems. Apparently, Motilal Nehru had invited a large number of non-Kashmiris, including some Muslims. In orthodox Kashmiri families, it was taboo in those days to sit and eat with non-Kashmiris. Kamala's parents, of a more orthodox hue, were afraid that their friends would take umbrage. Finally, they decided that they would not invite anyone at all. As it turned out, Motilal's guests were so many that the absence of friends of the bride's family was not noticed.[2]

The sensitivity of Kamala's parents to the Kashmiri community's feelings was understandable. The first Kashmiri pandit had probably migrated to Delhi in the reign of Shah Jahan. The Kashmiri brahmins were proficient both in Sanskrit and Persian, and were ideal employees in *daftar* (office) and durbar. Their talents were found useful both by the Mughal court and the British administration. Not surprisingly, by the turn of the nineteenth century, there was a considerable Kashmiri pandit community in Shahjahanabad concentrated, almost without exception, in the small area in and around Sita Ram Bazaar. Indeed, a small but significant street off Sita Ram Bazaar is still named Gali Kashmirian. The more wealthy and influential Kashmiri migrants built impressive havelis; some of these mansions—Sheesh Mahal, Mahalsara and Chhoti (small) haveli— are still remembered by older residents. Kamala's parents were thus— both in physical and cultural terms—part of a compact ethnic community, and were obliged to follow its zealously guarded code of ethics, unlike the Nehrus, who in distant Allahabad, could afford to shed some of the community's orthodoxies in preference to Western values and style of living.

The Haksar haveli remained with the family till the mid-seventies, when it was sold to the Delhi Yarn Association. The rich cloth merchants of the association wanted to use the premises for some charitable purpose. They toyed with the idea of converting it into a hospital or a *dharmshala*. However, before anything could be implemented, a property dispute within the association froze all

New structures now overlook the inside of the haveli.

plans. For the last decade and a half the haveli has stood unoccupied, unutilized and unmaintained, disintegrating into rubble and ruin, bit by bit.

Today it is hardly visible from the Sita Ram Bazaar. A row of shops have covered the mansion's periphery. Parts of the property's outer wall caved in in 1985 due to lack of upkeep. The Yarn Association agreed with the shopkeepers that it would be best to demolish the wall entirely. However, the beautiful pink stone gate still stands; the two handsome fish engraved on it, and the delicate jharokha above, still compel attention, although one part of the structure is almost hidden by a huge hoarding. An ugly collapsible steel barrier prevents entry into the haveli from the main gate. A side entrance and a narrow, steep staircase leading from it take one in.

OPPOSITE:

A forgotten past. A new generation.

RIGHT:

Glimpses of an earlier grandeur.

125

Arches amidst the rubble.

Inside, the ruins speak of a past grandeur. A few stone pillars stand in isolation; others are strewn around. Huge rafters lie scattered. Some arches remain, evidence of the wide daalans that once surrounded the inner courtyards. Hardly any of the walls survive. From the height of one or two that have not fallen, the original three-storeyed structure of the building can be gauged. The tehkhana can also be seen, but it is so full of rubble and filth that it is difficult to enter. The haveli premises are unusually quiet, the noise of the street somehow kept at bay. One can imagine how much more peaceful it would have been in the days when Sita Ram Bazaar was not the busy street it is now.

Today, a halwai (cook) uses a part of the Haksar haveli to prepare meals for weddings. Huge utensils give a surreal touch to the ruins. The cook, who hails from Madhya Pradesh, has been a regular tenant for several years. He does not know of the history of the building. Once a month, he says, the *munim* (clerk) of the landlords comes to collect the rent and he pays promptly.

NOTES

1   Henny Sender, *The Kashmiri Pandit*, Delhi, 1988.
2   Kamla Nehru's brother, C. B. Koul's oral testimony, transcript, Jawahar Lal Nehru Memorial Library, New Delhi.